What others are saying about this book:

"So, at three o'clock in the morning I arose and revised my notes as much as possible to the DUTTON SUPERIOR SPEECH FORMULA. I know this made it a better talk. The audience reaction confirmed it." George Romney, formerly CEO of American Motors Corp., Governor of Michigan and Secretary, United States Department of Housing and Urban Development.

"John Dutton has done his homework on this book. It is one of the best-researched books on the subject of speaking that I've found. Whether it's understanding audience behavior or handling stage fright, John makes it easy to get the information you need. This is a book that every speaker's library ought to have." Michael A. Aun II, 1978 World Champion of Public Speaking for Toastmasters International, South Carolina.

"It helps people overcome what most of them are afraid of. . . . If it were sold as a self study course through the American Management Association or the American Institute of CPAs, it would probably sell for $95." Ronald Roberts, CPA, Wisconsin.

"Such a simple, clear explanation of a complex subject! I read it in two hours and I'm not a fast reader!" Diana Lewis, director, VOLUNTEER—The National Center, Louisiana.

"This book is user friendly. It presents speaking as something 'doable.' Just about anybody could read this book and become a good speaker with practice." Martha Dealey, associate manager, Texas.

"This is truly a masterful book of sound helpfulness. It is also much more. There are guidelines for believing — in faith and hope — that we can rise above our more ordinary expectations for ourselves." Elmer Otte, president, Retirement Research, Wisconsin.

"The eight trade secrets are great. I really learned a lot more than I usually do reading this type of book." Greg Smith, lawyer, Maryland.

"The step-by-step approach and the usable, practical suggestions will make How To Be An Outstanding Speaker *a valuable addition to the library of today's successful professional."* Lester Stroh Jr., church executive, Missouri.

"It is different, of course, from standard fare public speaking books. The technical aspects of audience attention and how to increase attentiveness were real eye openers." Mike Baarts, salesman, Wisconsin.

How To Be An Outstanding Speaker

EIGHT SECRETS TO SPEAKING SUCCESS

by: John L. Dutton

LIFE SKILLS PUBLISHING COMPANY, NEW LONDON, WISCONSIN

THIS IS AN AMERICAS BOOK
PUBLISHED BY LIFE SKILLS

Life Skills Publishing Company
Post Office Box 282
New London, Wisconsin 54961

Library of Congress Card Catalog Number
85-81399

ISBN: 0-9615335-5-2

Printed in the United States of America

TABLE OF CONTENTS

"... we simply have to do whatever comes our way to the best of our abilities. And trust that God will find His way to touch someone else with them."

—Henry Winkler, The Fonz

ACKNOWLEDGEMENTS

The thoughts and encouragement of colleagues, friends and family made this book much better. The names of many are listed below with gratitude and pride.

Kenn Allen
Mike Baarts
Marilyn Beyer
Robert Christiaansen
Rudy Brunner
Steve Clapp
Judy Davinich
Martha Dealey
Charles Dull
Audrey Dutton
James Dutton
John Dutton II
Velma Dutton
Mary Eisch
Rev. Stephen Ellerbusch
Mark Femal
David Fiess
Sidna Geyer
William Grimm
Sally Hays
Melvin Kieschnick
Mike King
Theodore Kleinhans
Susan Knaack
Rev. Martin Koehneke
Dale Krause

Robert Lane
Cheryl Lambert
Gary Larsen
Diana Lewis
Patti Lowery
Arthemise Luke
Jerry McCole
Greg Michaelson
Doug Mosel
Elmer Otte
Maija Penikis
Ronald Roberts
The Hon. George Romney
Kay Saunders
Diane Seiltz
Allan Skruby
Gregory Smith
Mary Smith
Phil Snyder
Stephen Snyder
Dale Stratton
Lester Stroh Jr.
David Tetzlaff
Wilbur Tewes
Michael Walter
Marlene Wilson

Cover Design and Artwork: David Kapszukiewicz
Cover Illustration: Jeff Hargreaves
Typesetting: The Composing Room

"Our chief want in life is somebody who will make us do what we can."

—Emerson

FOREWORD

As a youthful missionary and lifetime church leader, trade association executive and corporate chief executive officer, governor and cabinet member, civil leader and Chairman of VOLUNTEER—The National Center, I have given countless talks. As a student I took speech classes and after college read a number of books on making a good talk. Many of my speeches produced standing ovations.

But I had an unexpected experience in reading the manuscript copy of this book by John Dutton. I read it on an evening airplane flight taking me to give a breakfast time address the next morning at a national convention of newspaper executives in Salt Lake City. My assigned topic was, "Achieving New Levels of Management." The subject was well within my experience. Furthermore, I had prepared my talk well in advance. I felt confident and satisfied with its content.

After reading John's book I came to these conclusions:

1. His "how to" suggestions were consistent with what I knew about giving a good talk, and

2. He made suggestions beyond those I had previously learned from study and my own speech experience.

His book convinced me immediately that I could improve my talk for the next morning by conforming to the "Dutton Superior Speech Formula" in chapter two. I arrived in Salt Lake City late at night and went right to bed, but I couldn't stop thinking of how this book's suggestions would improve my previously prepared talk. So, at three o'clock in the morning I arose and revised my speech notes to conform as much as possible to the DUTTON SUPERIOR SPEECH FORMULA.

I know this made it a better speech. The audience reaction confirmed it.

Without hesitation or qualification I can recommend this book as superior to anything I have previously read or heard about giving an effective speech. I know its methods work.

GEORGE W. ROMNEY

Mr. Romney has served as chief executive officer of American Motors Corporation, governor of the State of Michigan and secretary of the United States Department of Housing and Urban Development.

Introduction

Using the ideas in this book, most people can become better speakers than 90 percent of the people they know. This section shows you why that seemingly incredible claim is actually very possible. It also paints a picture of the speaker I think you can be.

"Dost thou love life? Then do not squander time, for that is the stuff that life is made of."

—Benjamin Franklin

INTRODUCTION

First of all, congratulations for being the kind of person who is interested enough in yourself and your future to begin a book like this. Most people aren't, as you know.

You may be a good speaker already, someone for whom this book will be a source of a few extra tips. That's good! I want this book to be extremely helpful to you.

On the other hand, you may be feeling uncertain . . . wondering if this is really going to "work" and if it will be worth your time. Maybe you're even glad that only a few people know you're reading this. If so, that's nothing to worry about or be ashamed of; I started with those feelings myself. In 1962 I was a self-conscious, stumbling speaker who hated to talk before a class or group. Over the years I had experiences and jobs that helped me discover and develop a special way to go about giving talks that produced dramatic results and changed my life. In recent years I've received standing ovations after giving 40 minute motivational speeches on a stage without notes.

In this book I want to share my "special way" with you. It is a way that can help most people become better speakers than 90 percent of the people they know. This may seem impossible at first. It is not, simply because almost everyone follows the common sense notion that we acquire speaking skills just like we learned to walk, automatically and with no special effort. They act on the belief that speakers are born, not made; that if you don't have speaking talent, forget it; and that adults rarely learn new tricks. This is simply not true. Highly respected people who started out as poor speakers and developed considerable skill include Dr. Norman Vincent Peale and Sir Winston Churchill.

If you have average talent and motivation and if you make a reasonable investment of time and energy, you may soon be recognized as being among the best speakers in your community, professional association, volunteer organization or corporation.

The idea of being among the best in your group or community is more than a casual comment or wild claim. People do not evaluate performance by comparing it against an absolute standard; they engage in what the distinguished psychologist Leon Festinger calls "social comparison," which means they judge themselves (and you) in relation to the rest of the group or others they happen to know.* "Among the best" also means that you *can* be much better than merely good enough to avoid embarrassment or good enough to get by. This system has produced dramatic results for others; and it can do the same for you.

I also want to be honest with you and I encourage you to be honest with yourself, about some things this "special way" will not do. While it can help most people, it will not help everyone. It is not a magic door to success or to the admiration and respect of others. In all probability it will not turn you into a professional platform speaker worth hundreds or thousands of dollars for each appearance. It may not provide answers to some unusual challenges faced by people like the clergy, who must speak at length to the same audiences every week.

But it *can* give you the know-how and power that will greatly increase your chances for drawing the best out of life in the years ahead! It is a way most people can become better speakers than 90 percent of the people they know. And it is almost certain that you are one of them.

*See reference on page 17.

THE FUTURE I SEE FOR YOU

In my mind's eye there exists a vision of the speaker you can be. It applies to speaking in business, volunteer and social situations. Reports from those who have used all or part of this speaking system suggest that it is a realistic vision, more than pie in the sky, more than fantasy. Could my vision for you be yours for yourself? Please think about that, because having it, wanting it and believing that it can happen will do much to make it come true.

As you enter the room the crowd is about what you expected, a few more maybe. You carry your folder easily under your arm and move toward the head table, shaking a few hands and exchanging greetings along the way. You introduce yourself to the chairperson. In a few minutes the meeting is called to order and you are seated at the head table with three or four others. As the meeting moves along, people in the audience notice that you are unusually relaxed and they wonder how you manage it. After a brief, low key introduction and some polite applause, you rise and walk calmly to the podium, carrying nothing in your hands.

You smile and adjust the microphone with the easy moves of a person who has done it often. Within three minutes you establish yourself as someone the audience can accept as a friend. Within five minutes people realize you are a person of substance with something important to say. You move into the body of your talk in a way that covers all your major points and holds everyone's attention. You don't wonder if you have their attention; you know *it, you feel it and they do too.*

Fifteen minutes later you move easily toward your conclusion which, like a magnet, draws people to your subject and to you. Your final words come off with a penetrating power that touches minds and hearts. You close with, "Thank you," and the applause is much more than polite. It's louder, longer and everyone knows why.

As you leave, people make special efforts to meet you and shake your hand. They thank you for coming. "What you said was so helpful." "I learned so much that will help me in my work." "It's good to know that someone is doing the planning and thinking about these things." "I know just what you mean." "I could listen to you for an hour."

The ride home is a joy. No need for the radio; in your head is the joyful music of your own symphony. You smile at yourself and for yourself. You're thankful for being asked to speak. And you're proud, so proud, to have done a good job. But when friends ask later how it went, you reply with only, "Fine, they liked it."

And Then!

You begin to notice that a few people at work have heard about your speech and how it was received. They seem more interested in you and more respectful. Somehow you get the feeling that people are taking some of your ideas more seriously than before, that you're more admired and appreciated. You begin to apply what you have learned about platform speaking to small group meetings and one-on-one situations. Your impact and persuasiveness continue to increase and you are able to be more helpful than before.

Then two people from an organization of which you've been a member for years call and ask you to accept the position of president. They talk about how they need a leader and that you're the person they want. You agree to serve. Back at work people again notice. Your boss comments with more than casual interest about your new position as president.

Sometime later your department is reorganized and you move up a level in the organization. People who previously saw them-selves as your equal now see you in a better light and offer their congratulations. Somehow they know you're different than before. Things continue to improve. There are new and more positive forces in the air!

All this didn't happen by accident, by luck or by taking advantage of others. You made it happen because you were helpful. You knew how to take advantage of a speaking opportunity so that it helped to change your future for the better. Very few people can do that, but you can and you did.

This vision or dream can come true over and over again in your life just as it has in mine. Public speaking makes it more likely because it enables you to make a larger, more effective and more generous contribution to the people and projects in your world. To put it in a word, you become more "helpful." These helpful people are usually the ones who get ahead in the world. And you can be one of them!

REFERENCES

Page
14 People do not evaluate: Festinger, Leon, "A Theory of Social Comparison Processes," *Human Relations,* 1954, pp. 117-140.

"The highest reward for a person's toil is not what they get for it, but what they become by it."

—John Ruskin

Trade Secrets

After reading these pages you will see
that there is more to the trade secrets
in this book than meets the eye.
Some of your "old friends" may
also mean more to you than
they did before.

"Wealth is thoughts, not things."

—Robert G. Allen

TRADE SECRETS

Every field or profession has its "tricks of the trade"— things that only insiders learn how to do. We love to watch these insiders because what they do is both fascinating and productive. Their tricks or trade secrets are like the "patterns" or "vocabularies" that Nobel Laureate Herbert Simon discovered in his fascinating research. For the past 25 years Simon has been working on artificial intelligence, trying to get computers to "think" as we do rather than conducting monstrously logical searches for correct solutions to problems. He centered his work on the game of chess and the fact that it is theoretically possible to teach a computer to play the game rationally. However, it is not possible in a practical sense, since eliminating all possible moves one by one would take hundreds of years for even the fastest of them.

Simon gave chess masters, the best players in the world, 10 seconds to look at a chess game in progress and then analyzed their mental processes. He found that, after the game was removed from sight, the masters could remember the position of almost every piece on the board. Further research revealed that the masters have familiar patterns, or in Simon's term "vocabularies," of games in progress, and that they work out of these in deciding which moves to make. Masters can recall up to 50,000 patterns; chess players one skill level below them have vocabularies of only about 2,000 patterns. However, players at all levels use the technique of asking questions like, "What have I seen like this?," "What worked before?," "What will work this time?"

This is very similar to the know-how and life skills we all develop as years go by. Simon is now calling them "old friends." They are the techniques, learned in school or with experience, that become one's treasured keys to success.

The following chapters will introduce you to eight of my "old friends." They are as familiar and trusted as the tools on my basement workbench that I have owned and used since I was a boy. They have been a key to the success I've enjoyed as a high school principal and now in my best ever job at Aid Association for Lutherans (AAL). They can become your old friends too.

Please don't be surprised if what you learn is different from what you may have read in other books about this. A few texts on public speaking mention some of them briefly, most do not mention them at all. Either professional speakers who write books haven't discovered them, or they aren't telling. I've learned most of them over 20 years by trial and error while giving talks about the high school in Philadelphia and about the national volunteer program I'm now responsible for developing at AAL. Some of them have produced such good results that I wondered if I was cheating by doing things differently from what I'd read elsewhere. Now I not only know better, I know why they work. After reading this book you will know too.

Before you begin chapter one, please consider one suggestion, which is that you adopt my habit of being careful about sharing these secrets with others. People admire and respect something more when the knowledge of how to do it isn't passed around as everyday information. The vast majority of people will be more casually curious than seriously interested in improving their speaking skills, so they wouldn't be helped by your revelations anyway.

After my old friends become yours, you may want to share what you've learned with a special person or two. That's fine, but select them carefully and see how they react to a few of the secrets before you reveal them all.

REFERENCES

Page

20 Wealth is thoughts, not: Allen, Robert G., *Creating Wealth,* New York: Simon and Schuster, p. 290.

21 For the past 25: Simon, Herbert A., *Models of Thought,* New Haven: Yale University Press, 1979.

22 Simon is now calling: Peters, Thomas, J., and Waterman, Robert H. Jr., *In Search of Excellence,* New York: Harper and Row, 1982, p. 67.

"If money is your hope for independence you will never have it. The only real security that one can have in this world is a reserve of knowledge, experience and ability."

—Henry Ford

CHAPTER 1
The Secret Of Understanding Audience Behavior

The trick in giving a speech is not to get it said. But to get it heard. This chapter will help you understand what goes on in people's heads when they are listening to a talk. Knowing this, you will be ready to learn how to design a speech, which is covered in Chapter 2.

"It's a complex world. I hope you'll learn to make distinctions. A peach is not its fuzz, a toad is not its warts, a person is not his or her crankiness. If we can make distinctions, we can be tolerant, and we can get to the heart of our problems instead of wrestling endlessly with their gross exteriors."

—Alan Alda

THE SECRET OF UNDERSTANDING AUDIENCE BEHAVIOR

Most public speakers design talks around their topics, rather than starting with some not-very-complicated facts about how people behave as listeners in an audience. What's odd about this is that people probably sense every one of these things when they listen to another speaker. But when *they* speak they seem to forget what it's like to be on the receiving end of a talk!

There are 10 things you absolutely must know about how people behave in an audience. After reading about them you may think they are rather obvious. You will probably notice that they describe your behavior in an audience too.

We'll take them one by one. The following two chapters show you how to use the 10 audience behavior principles to produce a speech that fits people, and that puts across exactly what you want to say.

1. CARRY OVER

Thoughts and actions in one event are influenced by what happened in a prior one. In an important and interesting experiment, Temerlin and Trousdale wrote a script of a fictitious interview with a relaxed, confident and productive man who had made an appointment with a psychotherapist simply because he was curious.* They hired an actor to play the role and tape recorded this "interview." The tape was then played for several large groups of subjects, each of which included law students, undergraduates, clinical psychologists and practicing

*See reference on page 43.

psychologists. In the experimental groups it was suggested at some point before playing the recording that the person to be interviewed, "looked neurotic but was actually quite psychotic." For some experimental groups this suggestion was part of the formal instructions; in others it was dropped as a casual remark. Control groups were either told nothing about the interviewee or that the recording was simply a "personnel interview." In addition, each subject was asked to write a descriptive, but not a judgmental, characterization of the interviewee. At the conclusion of the experiment, all evaluations were made without knowing in which group a subject was placed.

The results were astounding and somewhat scary. In the experimental groups that received the neurotic/psychotic suggestion, the interviewee was judged as being mentally ill by 84 percent to 100 percent of the subjects! In the control groups the mental illness diagnosis ranged from zero to 43 percent. Just as important, not a single one of the 300 subjects wrote a descriptive report of the interviewee; all were judgmental and not a single subject based his diagnosis on the actor's behavior!

The same thing happens when an audience listens to a speech. People are simply unable to clear everything from their minds merely because someone else is ready to say something. Their heads are full of everything but what you want; bowling tonight, the dessert was lousy, a before-lunch argument, a dentist appointment, washing the car, paying the bills, planning the weekend and a hundred more. All of these mental "tapes" are playing as "carry over" from what they were doing or thinking when you started. People can look right at you for 20 minutes and hear almost nothing you say, because they are listening to themselves and not to you. That's the bad news.

The good news is that the same facts of human behavior will help people accept later points in your talk because those points relate to and make sense in terms of your first ones. Also, people will carry over your ideas as they consider the presentations that follow.

THIS MEANS: IF YOU ARE GOING TO BE EFFECTIVE AS A SPEAKER, YOU WILL NEED TO BE ABLE TO BREAK THROUGH CARRY OVER TAPES AND TURN THEM OFF!

2. PROGRAM POSITION

Your place on the program will affect the impact you can have. The carry over explanation made the point that during your talk people will be influenced by what they've heard earlier, and that they will carry some of your ideas and suggestions into whatever comes next. Since what we remember diminishes over time, it follows that what is heard last, if it is well done, is generally remembered most, which is what you want. So, if you are asked when during a program you want to speak, the answer is usually the same; last, or as close to the end as possible.

For example, if a luncheon program includes awards, reports, business and your speech, try to speak last so that when you are finished the meeting comes quickly to an end. This gives you three advantages: You will be remembered best because you had the last word; you can refer to and use what has happened earlier in the program; and you will have ample opportunity to size up the audience.

Of course you need to modify this if being last would put you after a much superior speaker or a motivational film. In that event another rule takes over; speak before a better speaker or activity, or at the beginning of a very long program. Why? First, because following a better speaker or film is a sure way to be compared unfavorably. Second, because after a while audience fatigue becomes more important than carry over; you need to make your mark while people are still alert.

I recently had a rude reminder of this. More than a year ago I accepted an invitation to give a major address at a convention; without thinking I asked to be last on the program. Indeed I was! Before my turn to speak the 800 people in the audience had endured two hours of workshops, a one hour motivational speaker and a business meeting. As I was speaking those 800 weary people felt like 8,000,000 pounds hanging around my neck! Nice move, John.

THIS MEANS: YOU WILL NEED TO CONTROL OR AT LEAST INFLUENCE YOUR PLACE ON THE PROGRAM RATHER THAN JUST LET IT HAPPEN!

3.   SIDE TRIPS

When you *do* capture audience attention, you're not likely to
have it long. Paying attention draws heavily on a person's mental energy. People listen for awhile but then take side trips and
vacations into their own thought worlds. If your talk is only
average, most of an audience may "leave" and never return
until they applaud politely as you sit down. They will look right
at you, smile at appropriate times and yet hear only the first
minute of what you have to say.

In a typical experiment that tested performance, people did
the task but their attention wandered off to how others were
doing, to worrying about their performance and to repeating
choices already tried. Part of the reason something similar to
this happens in a speech is that we speak at about 130 words per
minute, while our minds process information at about 800
words per minute. We never hear enough from any speaker to
make full use of our mental computers. Before long we are
someplace else; a number of words and ideas have been missed
and we must try to pick up the train of thought all over again.
That's why it is necessary to listen repeatedly to a taped speech
before we hear most of it.

THIS MEANS: YOU WILL NEED TO KNOW HOW TO KEEP
AUDIENCE ATTENTION ONCE YOU HAVE IT.

4.   INTERPRETATION

Amos Tversky and Daniel Kahneman are international
leaders in the field of cognitive psychology, which in plain language is the study of how people reason or "think." They
found that people reason by using simple rules of thumb, and
by making both correct and faulty connections between
adjacent events. The scholars have organized their findings
around a number of major principles. One of these is the
principle of "retrievability"; we estimate the probability of an
event on the basis of the ease with which it can be brought to
mind. An example of this is that, if you give people two equally
long lists of names and ask them which is longer, they will

choose the list which has the most names of famous people they recognize. Another principle is that we are more likely to overestimate the risk of something unfortunate happening when a similar event has made a strong impression on us. For example, we are more likely to overestimate the chances of having a heart attack if a stranger dies from one in our arms, than if we read in the newspaper about someone who died.

In the same way every person in the audience will sift what you say through the filters of his or her own life experiences. We hear much of what we want to hear, especially if we strongly agree or disagree with what is being said. This fact of human nature can never be eliminated, but there are some powerful and constructive ways to influence it, as you will soon discover.

THIS MEANS: VARIED INTERPRETATIONS OF WHAT YOU SAY ARE SOMETHING YOU WILL HAVE TO EXPECT AND PLAN TO INFLUENCE.

5. LISTENING ISN'T READING

Burn into your mind a clear understanding of the difference between how people collect information when they read, from how they do it when they listen. Every time you prepare a talk, consider placing this sign directly in front of your writing table: LISTENING ISN'T READING!

You know something about this, of course. But it is utterly amazing how so many intelligent and mature people act as if they hadn't the faintest notion of it whatsoever! When reading, you are in control of repetition and speed. If something isn't clear, you can slow down and let it soak into your mind. You can think about it and even reread it several times. If a strange word is used, a dictionary can be consulted.

But when listening to a speech you have only one chance to understand. You literally have to catch an idea as it goes by. There is no slowing down, no repetition and no way to get clarity.

That's why a talk is absolutely and forever the wrong way to present complex and detailed information! Consider that, especially in relation to speeches in the world of work. How many times have you had to listen to someone give a report that was loaded with data and complex ideas? Everyone was quickly confused and bored out of their minds! That kind of information must be presented on paper, and only there! Detailed information can be distributed *after* you have finished speaking; your talk should focus on the larger concepts and trends to which the numbers and involved ideas relate. These include the relative health of the project or the organization, its major assets and challenges and its outlook for the future.

Simon's work on short term memory is directly relevant. In his work with chess players he found that people can hold in their minds only five or so "things" (letters, words, numbers, ideas, etc.) at a time. More than that and the mind gets confused; memory diminishes rapidly. Experience this yourself by trying Simon's simple research technique in which he gave himself sets of words and numbers and recorded how many he could remember. Then cast aside the foolish notion that your talks must have more ideas than that to be respected, or that your subjects are too profound and complex to be boiled down that far. The fact of the matter is that unless you are presenting a "paper" and everyone has a copy, people are going to keep clearly in mind no more than five things about what you are saying. And it doesn't matter whether the subject is nuclear physics, building a doghouse, how the company did last year or swimming!

Four Powerful Words

A speech is a place to present a few, simple, large and dynamic ideas that can be grasped as ear-to-brain information. Four words in that sentence are especially important:

Few: In a 20 minute speech you should try to present no more than three or four ideas or concepts, and these must be sub-points under only one thesis or major idea. Why? Because people have to work very hard at remembering five ideas and it's much better to present three they will remember than five they may confuse and forget. For much the same reason, use your time in a five minute speech to present one idea adequately rather than to rush through two or more.

Most people give speeches on topics they know much about. Amateurs usually try to say too much while the "pro" presents a few major ideas, makes a solid impact and sits down. Your heart will tell you to ignore this and say all you want, but your head must take control and hold you back from this psychological trap.

Simple: In giving a speech it is essential that you say things in ways that people can remember and explain to each other in simple sentences. Realize that if you wrote for reading what you are going to *say*, people would think you a simpleton. But that won't happen! Keep things basic and audiences will compliment you for being able to "talk their language." Here are a few examples of how to state the key ideas in a speech. Notice how the ideas in the speaking column are more like slogans, that they have considerably more "punch" than those worded for people to read.

Writing	**Speaking**
—Credit cards are a threat to sound family financial planning.	—Credit cards can wreck family budgets.
—There is a positive relationship between food consumption and body weight.	—Eat too much and get fat.
—The nation will have to choose between spending for defense or spending for	—It's either guns or butter.

domestic programs
that improve our
standard of living.

—The Surgeon Gen-   —Smoking cigarettes
eral has determined   causes cancer.
that smoking may
be hazardous to
your health.

—Boys adopt many of   —Like father, like
the habits and char-   son.
acteristics of their
fathers.

Does this mean that your speeches are to be little
more than emotion and over-simplified slogans?
Certainly not! The explanatory statements used to
expand on the slogans must have more substance, or
you will be dismissed as having nothing to say.
However, in doing this you must work hard to keep
things simple enough for people to understand and
grasp your oral explanations.

Thomas Peters and Robert Waterman wrote the
best-selling-ever book on our nation's businesses. In
In Search of Excellence they said that the excellent
American companies humanize their ideas beyond
simplicity to actually being "simplistic." If
organizations of this caliber find it effective and
acceptable, it must be OK for you and me.

How can you tell when you get it "right"? An
experience I had recently may be of help. I had
written something for this book which didn't make
sense when another person read it. She asked me
what it meant, and when I explained it she replied
instantly, "Then write it like that." Since that time
I've developed the habit of "working the words" in
my mind until a complicated idea "sounds" like I
would say it; then I write it like that. You can do the

same, or have someone else read your speech and ask you to explain anything that is not immediately clear. Then use your response to work out a clear oral explanation and rewrite the speech the same way.

Large: Simple does not mean tiny. Intelligent people won't tolerate speakers who waste their time talking about things that don't matter. Ears handle massive concepts, not details. They are the perfect means to learn about broad goals, fundamental directions, the meaning behind the numbers and the largest what, why and how ideas. For example, talk about the broad purposes and goals of your project or program, or the trends in your organization, and when finished distribute the details in a written report that the audience can review later.

Dynamic: Why do people listen to speakers when they could get more information faster without leaving home or office? A major reason is that a speech communicates feelings and emotions as well as factual information. It is a dynamic presentation that moves and flows with the values, commitments and energy of another person. It is face-to-face communication that calls forth an instantaneous listener response. If this doesn't happen, it simply is not a good speech! Every talk must move an audience in some way, even an annual business report.

Putting These Ideas To Work

I had been serving for several years on the board of a state-wide organization that had greatly expanded its annual convention. Attendance had gone from about 150 to over 700 in one year's time. The expanded program included a luncheon and luncheon speaker, 15 workshops, business meeting, awards program and an evening banquet. The preparations for the convention involved a score of people and a large number of procedures, forms and details.

I received an invitation to speak at a national convention in order to tell officers from sister organizations about our success. The people who invited me would have been satisfied with an interesting "speech," and that in fact was what they had requested. However, it seemed obvious that explaining the details of such a project in a speech would wilt the interest of everyone in short order. There had to be a better way to make good use of an hour on the program.

I asked several people to work with me in preparing "our presentation" (not my speech). The ideas and suggestions they supplied were simply excellent. Sorting through all our letters, forms and programs, we finally boiled them down to a stack of pages about an inch high. We used these in making a packet for each participant.

Next, we recruited "table leaders" for each table around which the 150 participants were to be seated. Each leader received an advance copy of the packet along with specific instructions about what to do. During the 30 minute table discussion each person was able to go through the packet in some detail . . . and have his or her questions answered!

My part of the program was limited to 10 minutes and divided into the following two parts:

1. A three minute introduction of the program, the table leaders and a slide/tape presentation about our convention.

2. An eight minute wrap-up. This presented the background and philosophical information on our convention, i.e., what our group was trying to accomplish, the major things we had learned so far and what we wanted to improve or change in the future. It also included a thank you to the audience for coming to hear our story and emphasized that we wanted to learn from their experiences as well.

THIS MEANS: YOU MUST AVOID GIVING LONG, BORING SPEECHES THAT ARE OVERLOADED WITH DETAILS; PRESENT A FEW, SIMPLE, LARGE AND DYNAMIC IDEAS THAT CAN BE GRASPED AS EAR-TO-BRAIN INFORMATION.

6. NONVERBAL COMMUNICATION

Nonverbal communication includes posture, where you stand in relation to the audience, facial expression (primarily what you do with your eyebrows and mouth) and gestures. An excellent piece of psychological research reveals the hidden powers of this kind of communication. When subjects were asked to decide whether a photo depicted a successful or unsuccessful person, their evaluations varied according to how the experimenter was expecting them to answer. Psychologists guessed that the experimenters were unconsciously influencing the subjects' scores by saying things that supported the answers they expected. In further checking, however, it was found that the difference started to appear on the very *first* photo the person was shown . . . before the experimenter had a chance to say anything about the subject's answers!

How could this happen? Experimenters did it by the number and length of the glances they exchanged with the subjects. Friedman says glances help people feel they are being treated with respect and interest, that they are having a successful "social encounter." Other studies show that the number of mutual glances between people drops after one of them gets a negative evaluation; increases slightly after a positive one.

Nonverbal communication also includes other actions. Chaiken and others videotaped teachers while they were instructing a 12-year-old in home and family safety. Those teachers who were led to believe the student was bright behaved differently than those who were told nothing, or told that the child was somewhat slow. With students they thought were bright, teachers tended to "lean forward more during the interaction, to look their pupils in the eye more, to nod their heads up and down more and to smile more."

Ironically, there is also an important nonverbal dimension in what we say. To communicate the idea of two people doing something, you could use the words "Mary and I," or "Mary Smith and I" or "The person with whom I." All describe the same two people engaged in an activity, and yet each communicates a different feeling or message about the relationship.

Most of what an audience "hears" is actually overpowered by what they see and sense. Harvard professor Gary Orren, an expert on the televised presidential debates, says this: "Whatever the good intentions that [the debates] be issue oriented, you talk to most well-educated people and their impressions are always in terms of 'strong', 'tough', 'weak', 'happy', 'sad.' Not whether he was right or wrong."

Because they are so subtle and largely beyond conscious control, nonverbal behaviors are also practically impossible to fake, or possibly even rehearse into natural actions. All of us have highly sensitive stink detectors that smell out "phonies" a mile away. That's good! It forces most of us to be honest and credible, to admit that we can't fool any of the people any of the time. However, we *can* give people the wrong impression about our words and ourselves if our natural nonverbal actions are overpowered by stiff, wooden behavior that is induced by fear, tension or lack of preparation.

THIS MEANS: YOU MUST ASSURE THAT YOUR NATURAL NONVERBAL BEHAVIORS ARE NOT SUPPRESSED OR HIDDEN, SO THAT WHAT PEOPLE SENSE WILL WORK FOR RATHER THAN AGAINST YOU.

7. AFFIRMATION

Peters and Waterman say it well, "All of us are self-centered suckers for a bit of praise." We know we're winners, and we're just waiting for the world to come around and catch on to what we know is the truth. When things go right we take the credit; when we fail we tune out and blame it on "the system." With affirmation our spirits rise and we exchange more glances with our partners; when criticized we look away. Praise gets us to feel better about our work than threats of punishment or, possibly, even money. We like to compare ourselves, not with our equals but with people whom we perceive as slightly better than we are. When we judge a partner to be competitive, rather than interested in helping both of us succeed, we become quickly protective and competitive ourselves.

THIS MEANS: CHANGE ATTITUDES AND BEHAVIOR WITH PRAISE, ENCOURAGEMENT AND STORIES OF PEOPLE DOING THINGS RIGHT; AVOID HARANGUES, PUT-DOWNS AND CRITICISM WHICH STIMULATE ONLY RESISTANCE AND REJECTION AND GET YOU NOWHERE.

8.   MEANING

How can I say this so you will grasp its gripping significance for your future as a speaker? Maybe this way: Victor Frankl was a German psychiatrist whose entire family was exterminated in Nazi concentration camps. He spent years in the camps himself, and saw a few men live while the vast majority gave up and died. After he was released, he wrote a book that has been translated into 38 languages; a book not like so many others about what happened, but a book about what people *thought* as it was happening to them. Frankl's enormous insight is that, more than anything else, we need meaning in our lives; things that make it inherently worthwhile to get out of bed in the morning, to get over our pains and to put up with the problems.

Journey into the hidden parts of your own heart, and you will find there your own desperate search for meaning. How do I know? Because I am searching too. Because I have spoken to thousands of people just like you; people who flat out love it when someone can put them in touch with the meaning of their everyday activities. Helping people find meaning is to give them one of life's greatest gifts, and to give yourself a "high" that can last for weeks.

The vast majority of speakers explain their subjects only in terms of such questions as what is it, how it is changing and how to do it better in the future. Sadly, they almost never answer the question that makes the answers to all others matter: Why is all this worthwhile . . . why should I give this a piece of my life?

There are scores of authoritative and wonderful statements that have been written about this; here are three:

"He who has a why to live for can bear almost any how."

—Nietsche

"In experiment after experiment Edward Deci of the University of Rochester has shown that lasting commitment to a task is engendered only by fostering conditions that build intrinsic motivation. In plain talk, Deci finds that people must believe that a task is inherently worthwhile if they really are to be committed to it."

—T. Peters and R. Waterman

"Man transcends death by finding meaning for his life. . . . It is the burning desire for the creature to count. . . . What man really fears is not so much extinction, but extinction with insignificance."

—Ernest Becker

THIS MEANS: WITH EXTREMELY RARE EXCEPTIONS, EVERY SPEECH OR PRESENTATION YOU GIVE (NO BUSINESS REPORT IS EXCEPTED) MUST HELP PEOPLE FIND MEANING FOR THEIR LIVES. THE QUESTIONS ARE SO SIMPLE, THE ANSWERS SO BASIC: WHY IS THIS IMPORTANT? WHY SHOULD WE TRY? WHY DOES WHAT I DO MATTER?

9. INTUITION

People reach conclusions and make judgments as much or more by stories as by analyzing facts and data. Tversky and Kahneman's research (see page 30) into the way people make decisions reveals that they do it by "feel" as much as by cold analysis. In the language of the street, they "trust their guts" as much as their heads. This is similar to what Simon reports about how masters make decisions in the game of chess. Searching for their "old friends," they ask, "Have I seen this before?," and "What is this like?" They latch on to mental pictures that make sense, as opposed to going through a detailed analysis of possible moves and resulting consequences.

These truths are not merely for the schoolroom and the club, they apply equally to the world of work. In *In Search of Excellence* Peters and Waterman say:

"As we worked on research of our excellent companies, we were struck by the dominant use of story, slogan and legend as people tried to explain the characteristics of their own great institutions. All the companies we interviewed, from Boeing to McDonalds, were quite simply rich tapestries of anecdote, myth, and fairy tale. And we do mean fairy tale. The vast majority of people who tell stories today about T. J. Watson of IBM have never met the man or had direct experience of the original more mundane reality. Two HP engineers in their mid-twenties recently regaled us with an hour's worth of 'Bill and Dave' (Hewlett and Packard) stories. We were subsequently astonished to find that neither had seen, let alone talked to, the founders. These days, people like Watson and A. P. Giannini at Bank of America take on roles of mythic proportions that the real persons would have been hard-pressed to fill. Nevertheless, in an organizational sense, these stories, myths and legends appear to be very important, because they convey the organization's shared values or culture.''

Daniel Isenberg of Harvard concludes the following in his article titled, ''How Senior Managers Think'':

''By now it should be clear that intuition is not the opposite of rationality, nor is it a random process of guessing. Rather, it is based on extensive experience both in analysis and problem solving and in implementation, and to the extent that the lessons of experience are logical and well-founded, then so is the intuition. Further, managers often combine gut feel with systematic analysis, quantified data, and thoughtfulness.''

THIS MEANS: WITH BUT VERY FEW EXCEPTIONS, STORIES AND ILLUSTRATIONS THAT CALL FOR INTUITIVE THINKING MUST BE A BASIC PART OF EVERY SPEECH.

10. PEOPLE ARE PEOPLE EVERYWHERE

We hear much about how people who live in one or another section of the nation are ''different.'' Rich and poor often have these ideas about each other, just as do the educated and uneducated, college professors and elementary school teachers, and farmers and business executives.

It just isn't so! The audience behaviors described above apply equally to practically all groups. People may value different things in life, and they certainly have different education levels, habits and traditions, but they have the same mental processes, and they are much more alike than different.

My travel schedule takes me to every part of the country, and there has been no need to adjust my speaking style or methods to differences that do not in fact exist. People are people and quite the same regardless of circumstances. They like straight talk, admire a helpful person with facts and know-how, hate to waste time or be bored, like puppies and babies and relate to the same kind of stories. If popular stereotypes ever were true, they are being erased by our national mobility and mass media.

THIS MEANS: YOU CAN AND MUST APPROACH AN AUDIENCE WITH THE KNOWLEDGE AND CONFIDENCE THAT THEY ARE VERY MUCH LIKE YOU. IF YOU AND YOUR SPOUSE OR A FRIEND THINK A TALK IS SENSITIVE AND REASONABLE, CHANCES ARE THEY WILL TOO. THINKING OTHERWISE RAISES DOUBTS AND TENSION, NEITHER OF WHICH YOU NEED OR WANT.

SUMMARY OF WHAT TO KNOW

1. When a speaker begins, people in the audience are still hearing "tapes" from previous events and discussions. It is important to break through carry over tapes and turn them off.

2. People usually remember best what they heard last; in general try to speak as close to the end of a program as possible.

3. People listen to speakers for a while and then take mental side trips . . . you will need to know and use techniques to keep their attention once you have it.

4. People will hear what you say through the filters of their own life experiences. This can be influenced but not eliminated.

5. A speech is a place to present a few, simple, large and dynamic ideas that can be grasped as ear-to-brain information.

6. We can give people the wrong impressions if our words are overpowered by conflicting nonverbal actions.

7. All of us are self-centered suckers for a bit of praise.

8. Every speech or presentation must help people find meaning for their lives.

9. People reach conclusions and make judgments as much or more by stories as by analyzing facts and data.

10. All people are much the same regardless of circumstances.

REFERENCES

Page

26 It's a complex world: Alda, Alan. "Dig Into the World." *Reader's Digest,* May 1981, p. 84.

27 In an important and: Temerlin, M., and Trousdale, W. W., "The Social Psychology of Clinical Diagnosis," *Psychotherapy; Theory, Research and Practice,* 1969, 6, pp. 24-29.

30 In a typical experiment: Marlett, N. J., and Watson, D., "Test Anxiety and Immediate or Delayed Feedback in a Test-Like Avoidance Task," *Journal of Personality and Social Psychology,* 1968, 8, pp. 200-203.

30 Amos Tversky and Daniel: Tversky, Amos, and Kahneman, Daniel, "Judgment Under Uncertainty: Heuristics and Biases, *Science,* September 1974, pp. 1124-1130.

32 Experience this yourself by: Simon, Herbert A., *Models of Thought,* New Haven: Yale University Press, 1979, p. 52.

34 In *In Search of:* Peters, Thomas J., and Waterman, Robert H., *In Search of Excellence,* New York: Harper and Row, 1982, p. 65.

37 When subjects were asked: Rosenthal, R., *Experimenter Effects in Behavioral Research,* New York: Appleton-Century Crofts, 1966, pp. 287-291.

37 Friedman says glances help: Friedman, N., *The Social Nature of Psychological Research: The Psychological Experiment as a Social Interaction,* New York: Basic Books, 1967, p. 56.

37 Other studies show that: Exline, R. V., and Winters, L. C., "Affective Relations and Mutual Glances in Dyads," In Tonkins,

S. S. and Isard, C. C., *Affect, Cognition and Personality,* New York: Springer, 1965.

37 Chaiken and others videotaped: Chaiken, A. L., Sigler, E., and Derlega, V. J., "Nonverbal Mediators of Teacher Expectancy Effects," *Journal of Personality and Social Psychology,* 1974, pp. 144-149.

37 Ironically, there is also: Wiener, M., and Mehrabian, A., *Language Within Language: A Channel in Verbal Communication,* New York: Appleton-Century Crofts, 1968, p. 31.

38 Harvard professor Gary Orren: Fink, David, "Cram Course: What to Say, How to Say It, *USA Today,* Oct. 5, 1984, p. 1.

38 "All of us are: Peters, Thomas, and Waterman, Robert H. Jr., *op. cit.,* pp. 55 and 58.

38 With affirmation our spirits: Exline, R. V., and Winters, L. C., *op. cit.*

38 Praise gets us to: Deci, Edward L., "The Effects of Contingent and Noncontingent Rewards and Controls on Intrinsic Motivation," *Organizational Behavior and Human Performance,* 8, 1972, pp. 217-219.

38 We like to compare: Jones, Russell, A., *Self-Fulfilling Prophecies,* Hillsdale, New Jersey: Lawrence Erlbaum Associates, 1977, p. 134.

38 When we judge a: Kelly, H. H., and Stahelski, A. J., "Social Interaction Basis of Cooperators' and Competitors' Beliefs About Others," *Journal of Personality and Social Psychology,* 1970, 16, pp. 66-91.

39 After he was released: Frankl, Victor, *Man's Search for Meaning,* New York: Pocket Books, 1963.

39 "He who has a: *Ibid.,* p. 164.

40 "In experiment after experiment: Peters, Thomas, and Waterman, Robert H. Jr., *op. cit.* Also Deci, Edward L., *op. cit.*

40 "Man transcends death by: Becker, Ernest, *Escape from Evil,* New York: New York Free Press, 1975, pp. 3-6 and 51.

40 Tversky and Kahneman's research: Tversky, Amos, and Kahneman, Daniel, *op. cit.*

40 This is similar to: Simon, Herbert A., *op. cit.* pp. 386-403.

40 "As we worked on: From the book *In Search of Excellence* by Thomas Peters and Robert H. Waterman Jr., copyright © 1982 by Harper and Row, Publishers Inc., New York. Reprinted by permission of the publisher.

41 "By now it should: Reprinted by permission of the Harvard Business Review. Excerpt from "How Senior Managers Think," by Daniel J. Isenberg (November/December 1984). Copyright © 1984 by the President and Fellows of Harvard College; all rights reserved.

CHAPTER 2
The Secret Of Basic Speech Design

A "basic" speech is the kind you will give in all but the most intellectual and formal situations. This chapter shows you how to put such a speech together so that people will be actually *drawn into* the information and meaning of what you have to say. You're going to learn how to apply what you read in the last chapter in such a way that people will be literally "helped to listen" to your message.

"His usual method of teaching was to tell the people stories."

—Mark 4:2

THE SECRET OF BASIC SPEECH DESIGN

The vast majority of people prepare speeches like the tailor who made but one size and style for every customer . . . one suit for everyone from the largest man to the smallest woman. The beauty of his approach was that he concentrated all his attention on suit making; he wasn't bothered by "people problems." The tragedy of it was that he was not helpful because he had no buyers.

When people prepare talks and think only (or even 90 percent) about the content, they are exactly like the tailor. They are designing a speech to fit very nicely into the tidy organization of their subject matter. They are thinking about themselves and what they want to say. And they are headed for trouble. Why? Because the most important part of any speech is the listeners; without their attention there is no reason to be saying *anything!*

To be successful, you must begin with a clear idea of what you want to say, including the major points you want to make. Then you design the talk, *not* primarily around the logic of your subject, but around the psychological characteristics of your audience. You do this without destroying the logical flow of ideas in your message.

There is a way to do this that produces very favorable and consistently successful results. The secret is actually a *system* for organizing and presenting ideas in a talk. You can use it hundreds of times, as I have, without anyone every catching on to the fact that your approach is a pattern or system. It is tailor made for the human nature of an audience. It combines your natural talent with a technique that leaves listeners awed and wondering how in the world you do it. You will be able to use these ideas for every kind of talk except formal lectures or "papers." (Chapter four shows you how to handle those.)

This system will make most sense if you remember six important ideas from the last chapter on audience behavior:

1. People experience "carry over" and do not clear their minds when you begin to speak.
2. Listeners take frequent "side trips" and you have to recapture their attention.
3. Affirmation helps us to be more open and accepting of others.
4. A talk must present a few, simple, large and dynamic ideas that can be grasped as ear-to-brain information.
5. All of us desperately need meaning in our everyday lives.
6. People reason as much by stories as by analyzing facts and data.

DESIGN FOR A 20 MINUTE SPEECH

Figure 1 on the next page presents the design of a basic 20 minute speech that responds to these facts of human nature. Notice that the vertical line, explained on the left, is for high and low levels of audience attention and energy. Numbers over the diagram indicate time for each segment and track total time elapsed. The letters ("A", "B", etc.) will be used as points of reference in the explanation which follows.

POINT A

When you are introduced and first approach the podium, you will have everyone's attention. That's why point A is high on the attention scale. However, this attention is mostly curiosity; your audience is waiting to make a very early decision about whether you are worth listening to, or if they should take a 20 minute mental nap or side trip. They want your talk to be

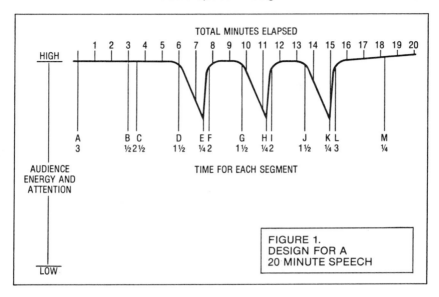

FIGURE 1.
DESIGN FOR A
20 MINUTE SPEECH

interesting and worthwhile, but they've learned through experience to wait and see.

Therefore, in the first three to four minutes of a 20 minute speech you need to do three important things with your listeners:

1. Turn off their carry over tapes.
2. Establish a relationship that gains beginning acceptance and trust.
3. Convince them that you will have something important to say.

How To Turn Off Carry Over Tapes And Gain Beginning Acceptance And Trust

This is not as difficult as it may seem; here's how to do it. After your first three or four sentences, people will make the decision whether to listen to you or take a nap or trip. That's why your opening needs to be practiced and practiced until you are programmed to do it with confidence and power. Just as important, however, is that your opening needs to be so interesting that your audience won't want to do anything but listen to you. And what is the most interesting subject in the world to your audience—every audience? *Themselves,* of course! Take a group picture, hand each person a copy and watch what happens. Every person will immediately ignore everyone else and find himself or herself in the picture first, just as you and I do. So, the openings of your speeches should almost always happen something like this:

> "Thank you for inviting me here today. It's a pleasure for me to be with you. (If it isn't, don't accept the invitation.) I want to thank you for taking time out of your busy schedules to be here. I'd like to get to know you a little better, so I want to ask you some questions about yourself, and also tell you a little about myself. First of all . . ."

Notice that all these statements, and obviously the third one, have the effect of reminding listeners that they are in charge, that the talk is responding to *their* basic decisions to attend. More than being grateful and polite, this sense of control helps increase the desire of listeners to invest the energy necessary for listening to what you have to say. Lefcourt divided people into two matched groups and asked them to solve puzzles while listening to a loud background noise. One group had no control over the noise; the other had a switch with which it could be turned off. The latter group solved five times as many puzzles as the former, even though they did not once turn off the noise!

Now continue with your introduction by asking the audience two or three questions such as the following:

- How many of us have lived in the states of Indiana, Pennsylvania, Maryland or Wisconsin? (Use cities if you've lived mostly in one state.)
- How many of us are parents?
- How many of us have had carpentry, horses or sailing (use your own hobbies here) as a hobby?
- How many of us have living parents over 70 years of age?

After each question, pause a few seconds for people in the

audience to raise their hands. Then say, "good" or "OK" in a tone that communicates your pleasure and approval. Follow by answering each question about yourself. For example, in answering the question about being parents, I mention that Audrey and I have two boys named John and Jim, and then I add a sentence or two about their ages and hobbies. I have fun doing this, and usually manage to poke a little fun at myself by saying something like:

> *"When we had horses I always picked up manure on Sunday morning before church. How many of you have done that? (Pause) Well, the rest of you haven't missed anything!"*

Or, in relation to the question about having parents over 70 years of age, I mention that my mother is over 80, and that we try to have dinner together once a week.

This question and answer period produces three powerful results. First, by getting people to answer questions about themselves you invade a person's consciousness and turn off his or her carry over tapes. Second, by expressing pleasure at being there, saying thank you and taking time to learn something about the audience, you send clearly affirming messages which help people to be open and accepting. Third, by answering the same questions about yourself you establish yourself as "one of the gang" and as a person they can probably accept and trust, at least to the point of listening with an open mind.

Notice the word "us" rather than "you" in the questions. Consciously use words that bring you and your audience together rather than push you apart. Also, ask only questions to which you can relate an experience and thereby identify with the audience. Remember that your primary purpose here is to turn off carry over tapes and build a positive, affirming relationship, not to collect or share information.

The Business Environment

If you're in a business setting, use the same approach but adapt it to the situation. Express pleasure at being invited to share thoughts and ideas. Thank those in the audience for their time. (If it's a required meeting, thank them for giving you their attention.) Then say, "I'd like to see how many of us have had some common experiences related to today's subject." Some business situation questions are:

- How many of us have worked on the XRYG computer?
- How many of us were here when (refer to something in the past that is related to your subject)?
- How many of us have taught grades one to four?
- How many of us have had experiences as a first line supervisor?

These work-related questions collect information and establish a relationship with listeners. If the audience senses that you are asking purely personal or social questions, the reaction will be negative. Work at developing questions that point up common experiences between you and your audience, and that collect information *having at least some relevance to the topic.* The benefits in terms of cutting through carry over, expressing affirmation and gaining acceptance and trust will be the same.

POINT B

How To Convince People You Will Have Something Important To Say

How much time in a 20 minute speech do you have for questions and answers? Not more than three to four minutes, because as you move toward minute four you need to achieve the third goal of your introduction, which is to convince your audience that you have something important to say. Do this by a carefully programmed *transition* into your first major point. This transition should conclude your question and answer introduction and prepare your audience for something serious. Here are two examples of how to do this:

"Well, it's so nice to be with people who are very much like me. Makes me feel right at home. That's why I think we are ready to turn our attention to something that's important to all of us. I've been involved with (mention your general subject) for some

time, and I've loved every minute of it."

"Well, I'm pleased that we've shared some common experiences as we've gone about our work. It makes me realize I'm talking to people I respect and, in a way, know very well. As you know, I've been working on the XRYG computer for two years, and I'm looking forward to telling you a little about it."

Benefits Of Transition Statements

Transition statements accomplish several things. First, they continue to pull you and your listeners together by talking about shared experiences and turning "our" attention to the subject. Avoid saying such things as, "Today I want to talk to you about . . . "; those kinds of statements separate speaker and audience. Second, the transition statement tells the audience that you are feeling as good about them as they are about you. Rest assured that everyone *will* be feeling this way, since the questions and answers are a good way for all present to rediscover that people are people everywhere, and are fun to be with. Third, the transition statement sends a quiet message that you are interested in being a helpful person. While you don't say this directly, and can't, people will sense it from your statements, and they should. Finally, observe that while we have *prepared* the audience for the major idea of the talk, we haven't presented it yet.

One Step At A Time

You may be wondering whether or not this type of introduction works when facing a hostile audience. The basic answer is yes, but it's important for you not to worry about this now. First, focus your attention on learning how to handle this kind of opening with neutral or friendly audiences. When you have learned those basic skills, you can apply them to less-than-neutral audiences, which are generally few and far between.

POINT C

Every speech must have a major thesis or controlling idea around which *all other ideas* will be selected and organized. It may help to think of your speech in outline form, with what you say at point C being roman numeral "I." You present the thesis or controlling idea in the two and one-half minutes allotted to point C. This is usually something like:

- We've had a great year!
- Drug pushers must be stopped!
- We need new industries in this town!
- Next year we need to work harder than ever!
- The XRYG computer can save you time and money!
- We had a balanced budget last year!

If people were like computers, we could simply announce our major ideas and they would understand and remember them forever. But they aren't. Their minds are flitting from idea to idea like bees in a flower bed, and they remember some things much better than others. How they understand and remember leads to another critically important idea you must burn into your mind: MAKE MAJOR POINTS WITH STORIES AND ILLUSTRATIONS FOLLOWED BY SHORT, PUNCHY STATEMENTS OF OPINION OR FACT.

When you are listening to a speech or sermon and your mind begins to wander, what snaps you to attention? A story or illustration, of course! When an address or speech is completed, what is it that everyone remembers and can repeat? A good story or illustration, of course! What will focus the attention of an audience on the essence of a key idea for more than a few moments? Stories, of course! What enables you, better than anything else, to show your deep commitments and feelings about something? What communicates conviction, sincerity and other feelings best of all? What reduces the tendency for people to *misinterpret* what you are saying? You know the answer!

The technique is far from new. Considering the reputation and stature of the one who used it best, it's a wonder that so few people have discovered it. More than any other person, Jesus Christ changed the course of history with His powerful message of salvation and eternal life. He did it not with library research, loads of historical data or endless analysis. He did it with stories like those about the prodigal son, the lost coin, the lost sheep and the 10 virgins.

MASTERING THE TECHNIQUE OF RELATING STORIES AND ILLUSTRATIONS WILL DO MORE THAN ANYTHING ELSE TO MAKE YOU A GOOD SPEAKER. Why? A speech is a personal exchange of thoughts *and feelings* between people! It's hot rather than cool communication in an age of television that has made us resentful of, and impatient with, impersonal messages. After all, when you've seen wars, riots, earthquakes, floods and executions happening live in your living room, who wouldn't turn off nice old Joe who rots our brains by rattling off nothing but cold facts and figures! That kind of "flat" speech wastes everyone's time! This certainly applies to business situations too.

Can you learn to find good stories and illustrations, and to tell them effectively even without notes? Absolutely, as you will soon discover!

So, this is what happens at point C:

- You use a story or illustration that leads up to your major idea or thesis. This communicates emotion and feeling and is therefore "hot."

- You follow this by stating your major idea in a short, punchy sentence designed for impact.

POINT D

Think of point D as item "A" under roman numeral "I." This is the first "content portion" where you explain and expand on your major thesis or idea. Plan to do this in not more than 200 words, or in about one and one half minutes. This is the time you have to communicate part of the actual content of your talk. THE SHORT TIME LIMIT MEANS THAT YOU WILL HAVE TO SELECT YOUR THOUGHTS CARE-FULLY, SEQUENCE THEM LOGICALLY AND EXPLAIN THEM BRIEFLY. This may be frustrating and difficult at first, since you will be tempted to share much of the considerable knowledge and experience you have acquired over time. You must *not* do that if you sincerely want to have an impact and enjoy the benefits of speaking success. To put the matter bluntly: Forget this principle, and you will fail every time!

Why? Because a speech is a vehicle for communicating only a few, simple, large and dynamic ideas. It's a way to convince people to read, on their own time, what you have written, or to motivate a few of them to talk later to you and others. So, plan on making your major point in one sentence, and on expanding and explaining it (again in words that are energizing and moving) in no more than one and one half minutes.

If you look at the diagram on page 49, you will see that as you do this, the attention level of the audience will *begin* to fade. Why? Because human beings simply do not find logical, information-heavy presentations all that interesting or even tolerable. Some of them will begin to hear their own tapes again, and a few others may even take off on a mental nap or side trip. However, since attention fades rather slowly, most of your audience will have heard most of what you said.

POINT E

Notice that point E arrives prior to when audience attention is lost. Before people drift too far into their naps or side trips you are going to *snap* them to attention again. Without them feeling one bit of resentment or frustration! Without them even knowing it! How are you going to do this? With a story or illustration! Both of them use intuitive thinking to emphasize and integrate the data or analytical information you've just presented! It works every time.

The stories or illustrations will be used either to explain or enrich your previous content, or to introduce and enhance what follows. The technique is to finish your content in point D, and then to move on with a transition like this: Finish your last sentence of content. Pause for about one breath (slightly longer if the story introduces the next content portion). Then say,

"That reminds me of when I was . . . ," or "An illustration of this point is . . . ," or "Now I want to tell you about. . . . " Notice that the attention level may not rise to what it was at the beginning. So be it. The middle of a talk doesn't *have* to be as powerful as the beginning and ending. An audience can't be on the very edge of its chairs *all* the time.

How The Pattern Or System Works

As you can see by now, the pattern is simply to alternate a story or illustration of about two minutes in length (points C, F and I) with about one and one-half minutes of content (points D, G and J). This will maintain audience attention at a relatively high level while you present your message. You may be surprised that in a 20 minute talk you have only four and one-half minutes for what most people think of as content or actual "information." Consider, however, that in a 30 minute television program advertisers also have very few minutes for their messages; the rest is entertainment. The entertainment time is the "price" companies pay for the privilege of having an audience listen to their content or commercial. Conversely, the commercial is the "price" an audience pays for the enjoyment of the entertainment.

It isn't how *much* time you have; it's what you do with it that counts. Your challenge is not to get it said, but to get it heard. Actually, you have a significant advantage over advertisers, because your stories are much more than entertainment. They are "intuitive information" that illustrates and powers your content portions. Advertisers can only plop their commercials into unrelated programs.

If you have 20 minutes, plan to present three segments of content in about one and one-half minutes each. The ideas at points D, G and J must illustrate and expand on the major thesis or controlling concept at point C. Don't present another major idea, ever! A speech works with one and only one major thought; all others must be supportive. Here's how you might do that:

  I. Point C: Drug pushers must be stopped!
     A. Point D: One way to do this is by better law enforce-
        ment!
     B. Point G: Another way is by educating our children
        about the dangers of drugs!
     C. Point J: We can succeed if we work together!

Another example:

  I. Point C: We had a balanced budget last year!
     A. Point D: One reason was that we held the line on
        expenses!
     B. Point G: Another reason was that our sales were up 15
        percent!
     C. Point J: Next year can be even better!

Remember that after each content section, points E, H and K,
you need to transition into the next story or illustration. When
you do these correctly, your audience will not be aware of them.
They'll come across merely as the next idea in your train of
thought.

POINT L

This brings us to the part of your speech that will drive home
and firmly establish your reputation as an exceptional speaker
and person. There are several things to be aware of here. First,
this is the last part of your speech, and as was mentioned in the
chapter on audience behavior, people tend to recall best what
they heard last. Second, this is the time in your talk when audience attention and energy will be highest. That's good, because
our goal is for it to soar right off the chart! Third, refer to page
49 and notice that the direction of the line ends in an *upward*
direction. A speech must always finish with high audience attention, and with energy rising. The idea is to conclude with a
bang, not a whimper!

And how do you do this? With your best and most dramatic
story or illustration. The one you've been saving for just this
moment!

I've been doing this . . . building my talks around my stories . . . for years. Sometimes I even adjust my topic to fit a terrific story I'm eager to tell. A few times I have found a completely new topic just so I could use a great story. However, I also felt uncomfortable about doing this; it just didn't seem to fit with all I had learned about how speeches were *supposed* to be prepared! Start with an idea, research it, make an outline, write the speech, etc., were the traditional lessons I had learned. And yet I continually received rave reviews; I figured I must be doing *something* right!

Then, in 1975 I received a Christmas present from my mother. It cost all of 50 cents, and was a book of sermons by a well-known preacher. People stood for hours waiting to hear him speak; they literally surrounded his church! Senators left their committee meetings to hear his famous prayers, which he delivered as Chaplain of the Senate. His ministry won him the love and respect of millions, and extended his influence across America. Mother's present was a paperback book titled, *Mr. Jones, Meet The Master.* Those sermons touched my heart and increased my faith as had few before; soon I was reading other books of outstanding sermons by this famous man, Dr. Peter Marshall.

In one of them I discovered something exciting and wonderful that I've never forgotten. While the normal procedure in sermon preparation is to begin with a Bible text and scholarly research, Dr. Marshall often chose a different approach. HE BEGAN WITH HIS STORIES AND BUILT FROM THERE! Stories are key ingredients in almost every speech; talks for some situations can be shaped to make use of great ones.

One Story Is Most Important

Remember, we said that at point L you want to finish with a bang, not a whimper, that you want to close with your best and most dramatic, powerful story. In almost every case the story around which you will center or develop your speech is the one you will use as your conclusion. How will you know when you have found the one story that is good enough? It has three qualities:

- It speaks powerfully to meaning or to the question of why, touching *your* heart, and probably stopping you in your emotional tracks the first time you hear it.
- It presents dedication, teamwork, persistence, creativity, compassion, faith, courage, etc., at its best.
- It has a dramatic or surprise ending, or you can find a way to tell the story to give it that.

As you begin or continue your speaking career, I think you will experience a "just can't wait" feeling to tell your best story at point L. This is the story that hammers home your major point, displays your allegiance to your ideas and ideals, calls others to be their best and leaves your audience with minds and hearts wide open.

POINT M

After the concluding story, the wrap up is simple. It goes like this: Say the last dramatic sentence of your story. Pause for two breaths. Then, say something that refers clearly and directly to your main thesis or idea such as, "Like I said, drug pushers must be stopped!", or "As I said, we had a balanced budget last year!" Then say a quiet "Thank you." and sit down.

The applause will take care of itself. Enjoy it!

Stories In Business Situations

Is this effective in workplace situations? Absolutely, as Peters and Waterman conclude in their widely-acclaimed description of America's excellent companies:

"In the end, whatever the source, myths are institution builders. The art of creative leadership is the art of institution building . . . And so, as it turns out, the excellent companies are un-ashamed collectors and tellers of stories, of legends and myths in support of their basic beliefs. Frito-Lay tells service stories. J&J tells quality stories. 3M tells innovation stories."

Why does this happen in enterprises dedicated to profit and serious business? It has to do with "intrinsic motivation" or the fact that people want more than money from a job; they want it to be worthwhile, to be meaningful. Few people can speak with as much authority and experience about this as does Edward Deci of the University of Rochester:

> "It concentrates on a person's perception of why he is doing the activity. When he is intrinsically motivated, the perceived locus of causality of that behavior is within himself. He is doing it because it provides him with some sort of internal satisfaction. However, when he performs the activity for external reinforcements such as money, he comes to perceive that he is doing it for the money. The locus of causality changes from within himself to the environment; . . . .In other words, the first process by which intrinsic motivation can be affected is a change in perceived locus of causality."

In a workplace presentation, the degree of drama or emotion may be less than for an address at a service club luncheon, a victory banquet or a dinner speech at a club. Shape and fit the degree of feeling to the situation, but *never* allow yourself to recite only dry facts and figures. If you do, you may miss the most powerful 20 minutes of your life!

Why 20 Minutes?

Because that is about as long as the well-prepared average speaker can hold the attention of an audience. If you are asked to speak longer, the best technique is to use any remaining time for answering questions. In fact, that's always something worth considering, because it gives listeners an opportunity to follow up on points of particular interest to them. The information benefits and psychological rewards of having one's own personal question answered are available only to those who come to hear a live speaker, never to those who only watch television or a movie.

The time allotted for questions varies with the time available, and usually falls in the ranges given in Figure 2 on the next page.

FIGURE 2: TIME ALLOTMENT FOR QUESTIONS AND ANSWERS		
Total Minutes **Available**	**Speaking** **Minutes**	**Question/Answer** **Minutes**
5	5	0
10	4 - 6	6 - 4
15	8 - 10	7 - 5
20	10 - 12	10 - 8
30	15 - 20	15 - 10
40	15 - 20	25 - 10

In Summary

Point A: Express pleasure at being there; thank your audience for taking time to attend; and say you want to learn something about them. Then ask two or three questions designed to bring you and your audience together. Say "OK" or "good" after each show of hands, and then answer each question about yourself.

Point B: Wrap up your introduction and convince your audience you will have something important to say with a carefully rehearsed transition.

Point C: Present your major thesis with a story or illustration, followed by a short, punchy statement of opinion or fact.

Point D: Expand on your major thesis or idea in about 200 words.

Point E: Transition into your next story.

Points F, G, H, I, J and K: Continue the story, content, transition, story, content, transition pattern as outlined.

Point L: Tell your most dramatic, powerful concluding story.

Point M: Say, "As I said, (repeat your main idea)"; follow with a quiet "Thank you." and sit down.

Allow appropriate time for questions.

DESIGN FOR A FIVE MINUTE SPEECH

The principles and design of the five minute talk are much the same as for the 20 minute presentation. Figure 3 below illustrates the pattern. The flow is as follows:

Point A: Say, "I'm pleased to be able to say a few words," or something similar.

Point B: State your major idea in a short sentence designed for impact.

Point C: Expand or explain the major idea.

Point D: Use a transition statement into your concluding story.

Point E: Tell a powerful story.

Point F: Say, "As I said, (repeat your main idea)"; follow with a quiet "Thank you." and sit down.

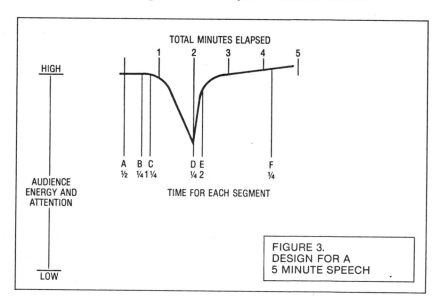

FIGURE 3.
DESIGN FOR A
5 MINUTE SPEECH

DESIGN FOR A 10 MINUTE SPEECH

Figure 4 on page 65 presents the design for a 10 minute speech. The flow is as follows:

Point A: Express pleasure at being there; thank your audience for taking time to attend and say you want to learn something about them. Then ask two questions designed to bring you and your audience together. Say "OK" or "good" after each show of hands, and then answer each question about yourself.

Point B: Conclude your introduction and convince your audience you will have something important to say by using a carefully rehearsed transition.

Point C: Present your major idea with a story or illustration, followed by a short, punchy statement of opinion or fact.

Point D: Expand on your major thesis or idea in about 200 words.

Point E: Transition into your next story or illustration.

Point F: Tell your most dramatic, powerful concluding story.

Point G: Say, "As I said, (repeat your main idea)"; follow with a quiet "Thank you." and sit down.

DESIGN FOR A MOTIVATIONAL SPEECH

Most of the speeches you've heard have probably been rather "flat" or short on feeling. Consequently, it may seem reasonable to conclude that the speeches presented above are actually motivational speeches that must be used only in special situations. This is not true, primarily because a purely motivational speech "flows" differently and is designed to achieve a different purpose. In many ways a motivational speech is a mirror image of the basic speech. Whereas the former uses stories to illustrate and power the content, the motivational speech uses brief statements of fact or content to illustrate and explain the stories. Its purpose is not to present information that answers questions of when, what or how, but to answer the question that makes almost any when, what or how tolerable . . . the question of why.

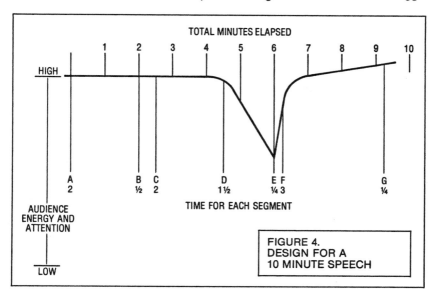

TOTAL MINUTES ELAPSED

FIGURE 4.
DESIGN FOR A
10 MINUTE SPEECH

Figure 5 on the next page presents the design for a seven minute motivational speech. It is included here for two reasons. First, to enrich your understanding and perspective of the basic speech. Second, to enable you to give motivational speeches at such a time as you have mastered the basic speech to the extent of earning consistently rave reviews. Don't attempt to give a motivational speech before you are able to do this, since it is considerably more subtle and difficult. The flow is as follows:

Point A: Express pleasure at being there; thank your audience for taking time to attend, and say you want to learn something about them. Then ask two questions designed to bring you and your audience together. Say "OK" or "good" after each show of hands, and then answer each question about yourself.

Point B: Introduce the story with comments that connect it to the audience and the situation. In two or three sentences answer questions such as why this group reminds me of this story, or why this story is important at this time.

Point C: Tell the story. It *must* be one of your best—the kind that stops you in your emotional tracks and has a powerful ending.

Point D: Explain in a forceful and usually a very quiet way how the story is directly relevant to the audience and to what lies ahead. Ask and challenge them to pattern their lives around what happened in the story, and provide affirmation by assuring them that this is indeed possible. (Be careful of gross overstatements here. In a motivational speech a little of this is acceptable, but too much is a "turn off.") Notice that these statements take the audience to higher levels of energy and attention than the story. Is this possible? Can anything but stories achieve this result? Certainly, because in this case you are using the statements to explain the story and to discuss the one thing that is most important to every audience . . . themselves. Design these statements so that your final comments are words of challenge and assurance.

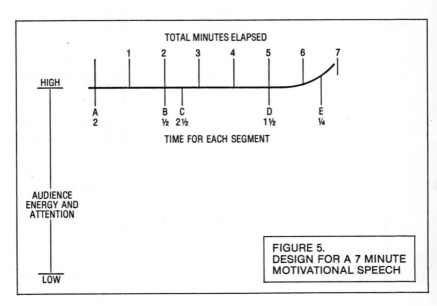

FIGURE 5.
DESIGN FOR A 7 MINUTE
MOTIVATIONAL SPEECH

Point E: Follow with a quiet "Thank you." and sit down.

BE FLEXIBLE AND KNOW WHEN TO QUIT

Three ideas are important. First, the times presented in each of the various speech designs are approximate; feel free to adjust them to your material and each situation. Feel especially free to adjust the time lengths suggested for stories by up to 20 percent either way. (A "two minute" story can actually be between 90 and 150 seconds long.) Be much more cautious about increasing the amounts of time you spend on content. While they can be expanded slightly (maybe five percent), the upper time limit is much less flexible. Why? Because audience attention and energy will continue to drop throughout the content portion, and after a time you will have lost the audience completely. This also causes great damage to your acceptance and credibility, which is the opposite of what you want.

Second, allowing appropriate time for questions may require that you use a shorter speech design than the time available. For example, if you have been given 20 minutes to speak, you may choose to use the design for a 10 minute talk and reserve the remaining time for questions. Your own judgment, and that of those who invited you will be your best guide here.

Third, notice that the speaking time in each design always adds up to slightly *less* than the time you've been given. That is not accidental. Try never to talk longer than your allotted time, and if at all possible use less. The goal is always to sit down *before* the audience thinks you should. You want them to feel sorry you're finished. Besides, everyone will know you're a "pro" when you do a great job in *less* time than you've been given.

SUMMARY OF ACTIONS TO TAKE

1. Design a talk primarily around the psychological characteristics of your audience, not around the logic of your subject.

2. Use the speech designs in this chapter; try to talk for a few minutes less than the time you are given.

3. Cut through carry over tapes by using questions that bring out some of what you and people in the audience have in common.

4. Make major points with stories followed by short, punchy statements of opinion or fact. Remember that people "think" in stories, and that stories are strong conveyors of meaning.

5. In presenting the content of your talk, select your thoughts carefully, sequence them logically and explain them briefly.

6. Save your best story till last; end with a bang, not a whimper.

7. Don't be reluctant to adjust your topics slightly to make use of good stories.

8. Consider using part of your speaking time to answer questions from the audience.

REFERENCES

Page

46 "His usual method of: Matthew 4:2, *The Bible.*

50 Lefcourt divided people into: Lefcourt, Herbert M., *Locus of Control: Trends in Theory and Research,* Hillsdale, N. J., Lawrence Erlbaum Associates, 1976, pp. 3-6.

59 Mother's present was a: Marshall, Catherine, *Mr. Jones, Meet the Master,* New York: Harcourt Brace, 1975.

60 In the end, whatever: Peters, Thomas, and Waterman, Robert H. Jr., *In Search of Excellence,* New York: Harper and Row, 1982, p. 282.

61 It concentrates on a: Deci, Edward L., "The Effects of Contingent and Noncontingent Rewards and Controls on Intrinsic Motivation," *Organizational Behavior and Human Performance,* 1972, p. 223.

CHAPTER 3
The Secret Of Finding And Telling Stories

When you're finished with this chapter you will know why stories are so powerful in a speech, what makes some stories better than others and how to develop a speech around them. You will also learn how and where to find stories for your own speeches, and how to tell them effectively.

"After gesturing for the boys to sit in a semicircle about him, the old man began to talk of how he became what he was. He told them how, over years of study from young manhood, every griot had buried deep in his mind the records of the ancestors. 'How else could you know of the great deeds of the ancient kings, holy men, hunters, and warriors who came hundreds of rains before us? Have you met them? No! The history of our people is carried to the future in here.' And he tapped his gray head."

—Alex Haley in *Roots*

THE SECRET OF FINDING
AND TELLING STORIES

Tales, illustrations or anecdotes will be the most persuasive and memorable parts of your speeches, and you need to be able to find and tell them on your own. To do this with understanding, you must comprehend what stories add to a speech and how they work in the minds of people in an audience. The following points have been made about how people make decisions and sense out of their everyday lives:

1. They "feel" as much as think, using simple rules of thumb and making both correct and faulty connections between adjacent events.

2. They look for "old friends" and try to relate present questions or situations to similar past experiences.

3. They need to believe in what they are doing, to find meaning in their everyday lives.

Stories can shape a speech to these habits of the mind much like a glove fits the hand. Here is why they do that.

1. Stories communicate meaning.

Meaning is more of an experience or a feeling than a fact, an insight or point of view more than information. We have it when we sense that our activities are part of greater-than-life movements, or that they help make the world a better place for others. Meaning is difficult, probably impossible, to grasp directly; it must be caught rather than taught. The meaning of a nursing home is not in the buildings or the budgets; it is in the story of old Emma whose life is sweeter because of it. The meaning of a computer is not in brilliant technology or the hardware; it is in the stories of how computers improve the lives of ordinary people in homes, hospitals and schools. The meaning of life insurance is not in money or policy features; it is in the stories of Jason and Cathy who didn't lose their college education and their home when their father died.

If those examples strike you as too simple or overly dramatic for a sophisticated person in a technological society, forget it! John Naisbitt analyzed the content of our newspapers and reported some of his insights as follows:

> "High tech/high touch is a formula I use to describe the way we have responded to technology. What happens is that whenever new technology is introduced into society, there must be a counterbalancing human response — that is, *high touch* — or the technology is rejected. The more high tech, the more high touch.

> ". . . Folk art is the perfect counterpoint to a computerized society. No wonder handmade quilts are so popular. Even country music's popularity is partly a response to electronic rock."

Why do stories communicate meaning? How does it work? After 20 years it remains unexplainable. But it *does* work, and the results are almost mystical. Touching the hearts of people you don't know, pulling out feelings you can't describe or understand (feelings they didn't know were there and can't find themselves), and then being sincerely respected and thanked for doing it is a *powerful* experience! It is also an experience that nine out of 10 people can have regardless of their personality styles, and an experience that all of us must handle with humility, responsibility and great care.

2.   Stories make trends personal.

It is difficult to relate to the "fact" of 25,000 10- to 12-year-old homeless children. However, when a great tragedy is explained in terms of a nine-year-old boy named Na Shun, we are moved to conclude that something must be *done!* It's one thing for a boss to say, "I appreciate all the work you've done this past year to help us be successful.'' It's another to say, "Let me close with a few words about one of you that illustrate how our success is really the result of individual people doing a faithful, dedicated job over the past year."

Tversky and Kahneman term this principle "imaginability" and report that the more we can grasp a vivid mental picture of an event or situation, the more we will be influenced by it. Important as they are in decision making and speeches, facts and data are abstract and require translation into life situations before they matter and make sense. They are what we learned how to use in school. Stories, on the other hand, usually make sense in themselves. They are the stuff of life. All of us have been living inside the stories of our own lives since the days of our birth. Is it any wonder that we love them so much?

3. Stories touch beliefs and feelings.

Feelings and convictions stand alone as the most elusive and difficult of all qualities to present in a speech. As you have probably noticed, the vast majority of speakers avoid them completely and present only information. If you try to communicate feelings and convictions directly, failure is almost certain. But *you* don't have to! The right story will do this all by itself; all you have to do is tell it. Courage, for example, cannot be presented and appreciated by dissecting it in detailed analysis. But this can be accomplished by relating vivid legends and accounts of persons demonstrating bravery in the face of danger and death. The story does the work, and you get the credit. It probably shouldn't work that way, but it does.

4. Stories strike a responsive chord.

Stories often strike what advertisers call the "responsive chord." In a 30 second commercial there isn't time to explain all the benefits a product offers. The technique, therefore, is to place a viewer in settings that stimulate one to call up desires or dreams the product could supposedly help fulfill. Often these are mental pictures of ourselves being the persons of our dreams.

In reality they are patterns of thought, some of our "old friends." Watch for all the TV commercials that spark images of being glamorous, popular, sexy, smart or whatever. Their goal is to leave our minds tingling long after the advertisement has ended, at least until we arrive at the store or showroom.

Does it work? Certainly! If it didn't, corporate executives wouldn't pay astronomical rates for television commercials. Stories in speeches do this too. They touch listeners' emotional chords and open their minds to what you have to say.

5.   Stories let others make your point.

Stories or illustrations enable speakers to let others emphasize important points for them. If you are talking about productivity, a story about the highly productive Sam Morris or Alice Penning will drive home the point better than you ever could with simple encouragement and praise. The effect is similar to making a point and inviting the audience to check it with a third person for accuracy and honesty. Also, after people have "listened" to Sam or Alice for two minutes, they will be much more willing to listen to you again as you move back into a content portion.

6.   Stories help people discover you.

We are turned off by people who focus excessive attention on themselves. You simply can't talk directly about your own dedication to, or belief in, a program or organization for more than a few seconds without sending negative vibes through an audience. Stories let you display these qualities in ways that are attractive and socially acceptable. Listeners catch on to the kind of person you are by the stories you select, and by the way they touch your heart as you tell them.

WHAT MAKES A STORY GOOD?

For the vast majority of people, life happens in ordinary towns, in average houses and at everyday jobs. Its gripping challenges sneak up on us as we try to remain faithful to our ideals and friends, make each day count, be patient with and accepting of ourselves and give a good day's work for a day's pay. While there are great and famous leaders, they usually succeed by mastering these basic challenges of life. And each one of them knows that success depends on outstanding performance by the rank and file.

Your stories, therefore, will generally be about ordinary people doing everyday things in extraordinary ways. They will center on such human qualities as courage, faithfulness, devotion, loyalty, generosity, tenacity, humility, love, caring and dedication to great ideals and goals.

Two Basic Tests

There are two tests to determine whether or not a story or illustration is good enough for a speech:

1. Will the audience be able to relate to it and put itself in the place of the people in the story? You will be looking for accounts of people in roughly the same settings as your audience. If you are speaking to a group of professional people, look for incidents involving those who perform high level functions or information-based tasks. If the audience is a church group, center your search on people who are exceptional because of what they have done for others out of faith and devotion. Stories for a service club talk might focus on people who have made outstanding contributions in business or to the community.

2. Is the human dimension I want to emphasize presented in extraordinary ways? The best story is one that forces the book or paper into your lap, and leaves you pondering its meaning and significance for your own life and work . . . the kind you want to share with a special friend. Remember that's the *best* story, the kind you want for your conclusion. Obviously, there aren't very many of this caliber to be found; most stories will be similar, except that they will produce a weaker internal reaction.

FIT THE SPEECH TO THE STORY

Generally, you want stories having a reasonable relationship to both your topic and outline. But don't settle too firmly on your outline until you have selected the stories, and DON'T be reluctant to shape your content somewhat in order to be able to use a good story.

A common occurrence in my experience is to be looking for a story when my attention is attracted, not to a complete and well-written incident, but to merely a paragraph or two beneath which is obviously hidden a great drama. Or maybe something happens in my family that isn't a good story "as is," but it could be made good by creating the right situation around it. The challenge then is to use *creative imagination* to enrich and fill in the details. Give yourself artistic permission to do what is necessary to make your point, being careful not to cross the line into inventing complete situations for your own convenience, or distorting the essential facts beyond reason. The idea is to add helpful details without changing the essence of something you've seen, read or heard.

An Actual Experience

A few years ago I read something like this in *Branching Out,* AAL's magazine for its volunteer leaders of local branches.

> Branch 6218 in Homer, Texas, raised $10,000 for a Texas family of four after their home and all possessions were destroyed by fire last August. Insurance replaced only half the cost of a new home. Parents and two children were living with relatives temporarily. The local branch sponsored a series of bake sales and two fashion shows to raise the money. When presented with the check the mother said, "It's hard to talk at a time like this. We never realized we had so many friends. Our whole family is deeply grateful for your kindness and help."

I used that story as follows in several speeches at AAL conventions:

"Let's go to the town of Homer, Texas. It's only 8:30 on an August morning, but already you know it's going to be a hot

one. Except that won't matter much, because you are now standing between two firemen with a dripping hose, looking at what used to be your home. It's all black and smoking now . . . all the windows broken out. Your clothes and furniture are gone too. Jim and Tammy used to have toys, but not any more.

"Well, you say thanks to a few people who come by to help, and walk to your mother's home a few blocks away. Your wife and children are waiting, and there are hugs and tears all around. After coffee and some consolation to help the kids know that everything will be OK, you call the insurance man. The news is bad; you'll get only enough money to pay off the mortgage, which was for about half of what it will cost to build a new home. Things go from bad to worse, and hopelessness sets in.

"A week later you find that some of your friends belong to something called an AAL branch, and that they have organized five bake sales and two fashion shows to raise money for your new home. You watch with wonder for two months as people jump at the chance to help, and assure you that they are getting more out of it than you are. One day they come to your home and give you a check for $10,000.

"All the things you had planned to say at this time don't come out. It's quiet in the kitchen; even the kids are silent as they hang on to their usual spot on your leg. Finally, you wipe away a tear and say, 'It's hard to talk at a time like this. We never realized we had so many friends. Our whole family is deeply grateful for your kindness and help.' "

SPEECH DEVELOPMENT UNDER ACTUAL CONDITIONS

So you will understand how speech development works in the real world, let's pretend you are going to give a 20 minute talk on drug abuse to a service club. (The process for a workplace speech is identical.) You review the summary on page 62 and the design for a 20 minute speech, which is shown again in

Figure 1 on the next page. You find that you need the following major "segments" to assemble the talk:

Point C: Major thesis or controlling idea,

Point C: Story to illustrate the major thesis,

Point D: First supporting point and content for it,

Point F: Story to explain point D or introduce point G,

Point G: Second supporting point and content for it,

Point I: Story to explain point G or introduce point J,

Point J: Third supporting point and content for it,

Point L: Story for the conclusion.

You decide to center your talk around the major idea that "Drug Pushers Must Be Stopped!," largely because your own children have come home from school with reports of kids on drugs and how easy they are to buy. You have been to several meetings on the subject, and have recently taken the time to read and save three or four magazine articles about it.

You develop the general idea of the talk with these points in mind, and you write the following outline in a note to yourself:

I. Drug pushers must be stopped! (Major thesis for point C)

    A. The problem is serious! (Supporting idea for point D)

    B. Police departments need our support! (Supporting idea for point G)

    C. Family discussions about drugs are essential! (Supporting idea for point J)

One of your articles has a powerful account of how a boy with a great future was led to mental and physical ruin by terribly unscrupulous pushers. Since this story answers the question of "why" and communicates meaning and urgency, you decide to use it at point L for the conclusion. Also, the chief of police in your town spoke at one of the meetings you attended. You decide that his call for help, what his officers are doing, and how you and your friends reacted positively would make a good illustration at point F . . . something to introduce the content portion at point G. However, for the remaining two stories at

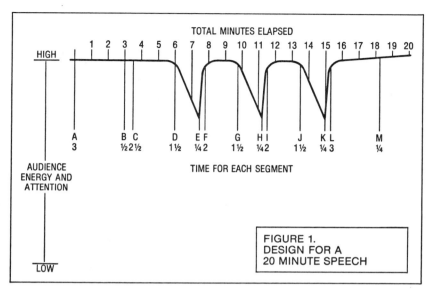

FIGURE 1.
DESIGN FOR A
20 MINUTE SPEECH

points C and I you repeatedly draw a blank, and are at a loss about what to do. In your mind the outline looks like this:

Point C: Major thesis: Drug pushers must be stopped!

Point C: Story: *NOTHING.*

Point D: First supporting idea: The problem is serious!

Point F: Story: Police chief's report and call for help.

Point G: Second supporting idea: Police departments need our support!

Point I: Story: *NOTHING.*

Point J: Third supporting idea: Family discussions about drugs are essential!

Point L: Story for conclusion: Boy devastated by pushers.

Solving The Problem

Here are your next steps to the problem of finding two more stories:

1. Go back and read through your articles again and determine if they contain any material you could use.

2. Skim the magazines and books in your home to determine if they happen to have any relevant articles or stories that might be helpful.

3. Visit the library and look over the magazines there.

Let's say this produces another good but not great story about a family ruined by drugs the children first received from others. The "others" purchased them from pushers who hung around the school grounds. You decide to use this story to give power to your major thesis at the beginning of your talk. Now your mental outline looks like this:

Point C: Major thesis: Drug pushers must be stopped!

Point C: Story: Pushers selling drugs near school.

Point D: First supporting idea: The problem is serious!

Point F: Story: Police chief's report and call for help.

Point G: Second supporting idea: Police departments need our support!

Point I: Story: *NOTHING.*

Point J: Third supporting idea: Family discussions about drugs are essential!

Point L: Story for conclusion: Boy devastated by pushers.

Changing Your Approach

Only one more story is needed at point I. You know there *must* be good stories about what parents have done to help their children stay away from drugs. But everywhere you look produces the same: Nothing! Two weeks go by, and you've been to the library twice without success. Tension begins to build as the date approaches. All you have for your effort is a good story about *another* police chief who has said much the same thing as the one in your town. That's the answer! You decide to use this story at point F.

This leaves the way open for you to use the results of a phone call to the chief of police in your town about what parents can do to help, followed by a call to the superintendent of schools.

This second call will give you information on what the schools are now doing that might be of help to parents. It also seems to tie in nicely to your opening story about kids getting drugs from pushers who were hanging around the school grounds. Therefore, your third "story" at point I will be a report about your call to local officials, and what suggestions they have for parents.

Final Speech Design

The outline for your speech has finally developed into this:

Point C: Major thesis: Drug pushers must be stopped!

Point C: Story: Pushers selling drugs near school.

Point D: First supporting idea: The problem is serious!

Point F: Story: Police chief from another town.

Point G: Second supporting idea: Police departments need our support!

Point I: Story: Phone calls to police chief and superintendent of schools.

Point J: Third supporting idea: Family discussions about drugs are essential!

Point L: Story for conclusion: Boy devastated by pushers.

As you reflect on your coming speech, you know it's not the perfect combination of stories you might have liked, but you have an outstanding concluding story, two that are at least average, plus one report on two telephone calls that will get the job done for point I. Not bad. You think to yourself, "By the time I'm done that audience will KNOW they have to do something about drug pushers, and they will know where to start." That's enough for rave reviews any day of the week!

THE PROFESSIONAL APPROACH TO FINDING AND TELLING STORIES

You'll be making real progress as a speaker when your search for stories becomes more of a low energy but constant process than one directed only at your next presentation. After you master this technique, people will wonder how in the world you can be so creative and clever. It begins with the realization that great stories to a speaker are like coins on the sidewalk to a child; a discovery, something always worth watching for and a reason for joy. I find my stories primarily in four places; family, work, magazines and casual reading.

Family

The years when children are growing up in a family are a rich source of stories. This is a time when youngsters are learning about love, diligence, responsibility, death, hope and confronting life in its largest and most basic dimensions. Their little successes, questions before bedtime and pride of achievement are all grist for the good speaker's story mill. I've told stories about my boys learning to ride horses, discovering that success in school takes work, loving me more after the death of a best friend's father and much more. Such stories can be used to illustrate a multitude of points about the challenge and drama of everyday living.

If personal or family stories are used to elevate one's self, however, the reaction is almost always unfavorable. Use them to illustrate another point in your talk, carefully keeping attention away from yourself, and the reaction will be powerfully positive. If you are an older brother or sister, a parent or grandparent, you have great opportunities for family stories; don't miss them!

I'm reminded of the time I was speaking to a group of people who were training to become teachers of other adults. We wanted them to realize that their attitudes and actions would have an enormous impact on their "students." We also wanted them to know that they were vitally important to the success of the whole project. To make those points I told this story:

"Last summer our family went to Shawano Lake and tried out some new water skis I bought for the boys. Jim and John had never skied before, and each was eager to be first to try.

Forty minutes later the whole situation had changed. Each of the boys had tried four or five times and failed. They were discouraged, and they suddenly noticed the water was getting colder by the minute. The whole outing was falling apart.

"Audrey looked at me and said, 'I think I'll try it.' As I helped her into a life jacket we exchanged some half-worried glances. Our unspoken but shared thoughts were, 'Is this really a good idea? You haven't done this in years, you know.' I could just see her paralyzed in bed with a wrenched back after this one.

"Well, she slipped into the water and soon everything was set. The boys were looking back as I gunned the outboard and the boat surged ahead. In an instant their mouths were open and eyes were silver dollar big. Mother was up in one try and gliding gracefully across the water with a smile and a casual wave.

"We made two circles and stopped the boat. Now the water was warm again and getting warmer every minute. Audrey climbed back into the boat and we went over all the basics once more. 'Keep your knees bent. Let the boat pull you up.' Believe it or not, John made it up on his first try. So did Jim.

"Who will ever forget that ride back to the shore! The manly pride of little boys was running high. But we all know that what made the difference was a teacher; someone who could tell others how to do something, and could show *them how to do it too. We all knew that mother was the true star of the day.*

"Teachers make all the difference in the world. That's why we are looking forward to what will happen as the result of your work in this project. Thank you for being part of it, and thank you for being . . . a teacher."

Work

Adults struggle with many of the same challenges at work as do children at home, and some of their victories are just as heroic. Accounts from the workplace frequently need to be anonymous and slightly disguised to protect privacy, but they are powerful nevertheless. If the people you want to talk about will recognize themselves as the subjects, or if others will, make contact in advance and secure permission to use the story in your talk. Promise not to reveal their identities. People will almost always be flattered by the attention; I've never been turned down.

An example here may help you find the stories or illustrations in your paid or unpaid (volunteer) work situation. When I was headmaster at Germantown Lutheran Academy in Philadelphia, it was important to point up the value of parents making sacrifices for their children's education. Simply saying it over and again, or giving *my* opinion, would have been an ineffective turn-off. What did work was simply telling the audience about two families in the school who were making such sacrifices and who were, as a result, raising outstanding children.

Magazines

You are likely to find a good story in any magazine you read regularly, but two seem especially suited to a speaker's needs: *Reader's Digest* and *Guideposts*. Both of these are most likely available in your library. Back issues there should probably be checked first, since stories a few years old will seem more fresh to an audience than ones which many people remember from last month's issue. If you are interested in subscribing, write to:

— *Reader's Digest,* Pleasantville, N.Y. 10570

— *Guideposts* Associates, Inc., Carmel, N.Y. 10512

Illustrations or stories in workplace situations can be found in the professional journals and magazines that are common to every field. Your search should generally be directed to articles published in the last year or two, since in today's world information and innovation quickly become ancient history. Remember that you are looking for stories about *people* confronting and overcoming challenges, not complicated technical reviews or formula laden reports.

Casual Reading

Whenever you read at leisure, you are in a prime spot to catch a good story. The Sunday paper, magazines in a waiting room and whatever you find in buses, airplanes or terminals can produce a winner. If you come across something you can't tear out or copy, jot a few notes on a scrap of paper and rewrite a better account when you get home or to the office. Don't worry about forgetting; if it's a great story, you'll easily remember more than you need for a talk.

HOW TO TELL POWERFUL STORIES

Storytelling is the most subtle and delicate technique you will master in order to reach your goal of becoming a successful speaker, and it is NOT particularly difficult if you apply some time and effort. You certainly don't have to be a ham or an actor to use stories or illustrations in a talk. That's because an audience is attracted to *any* story about people, and all you have to do is give them a two minute look into a real life situation. Here's how:

1. Focus on details.

Go back to the story I told about the family losing its home in the fire. Notice that it puts the situation under the microscope so that you can see and feel the details, the bits and pieces you would notice if you were really there. The newspaper said only that the fire happened in "August," but I said, "It's only 8:30 on an August morning, but already you know it's going to be a hot one." You were right in the middle of the situation, "between two firemen with a dripping hose." You knew the kids had no more toys. You walked to your mother's home and called the insurance company. These are all what a person would experience if involved in the situation. So, the first principle to remember in storytelling is to take your audience *into* the situation by helping them see the details they would notice if present.

2.   Stick to the topic.

Details can be overdone. If the story is about painting your own home, don't wander off into a long description of the various kinds of paint on the market today. Talk about your house, your colors, your equipment and *especially* about the feelings of those involved. Keep the story moving. It must have action and proceed steadily to the final description about an exciting event like spilling the paint or selling the house for a profit. Think about each sentence. Make sure that each one adds anticipation, detail or drama. Add whatever helps; cut everything that doesn't.

3.   Use intimate words.

When you talk to close and intimate friends, you use words suited to that relationship. When talking to others, your verbal style shifts to more formal language. Psychologists refer to this as "immediacy," and they note that variations in word usage indicate differences in the degree of separation from one person to another. The closer anyone is to us physically and emotionally, the more personal and intimate we are in our communication patterns. For example, if you were describing a strong marriage relationship to a business associate you might say, "Bob and Helen have a strong marriage; it's a source of strength for each of them." However, if you were describing this to your spouse over a quiet dinner you might say, "Bob and Helen are really in love. I can see it in the way they listen to each other, and do little things like pouring coffee and holding hands. When I see them I can just *feel* the strength of that marriage coming through!" The second principle, then, is to use words like the ones you select for personal conversations with closest friends.

How do you find these? By using your imagination! Think of yourself with a close friend in some quiet and cozy place. Call up those feelings of tenderness and care you have for that person; think of how you talk when your protective barriers are down, and your inner feelings and emotions surface. Then tell the story "to your friend" in that imaginary setting.

4. Talk slowly and softly.

Talk just as you would in that quiet place with your friend. When you start to tell a story, think of it as a break from the hard work of giving the content of your speech. Imagine yourself gathering the audience around you for a little relaxation, and the treat of sharing a yarn with someone special. You don't have to hurry, and you don't have to pound or shout; it's too important, too personal, for that. Use the conversational volume, pace and inflections that are part of your everyday communication with friends. When you do this correctly the difference will be apparent to you and your listeners. You will feel yourself relax a little in the stories, and move back into your content speaking style when you return to that portion of your talk.

5. Develop a surprise ending.

Work hard at getting a surprise and dramatic ending; as you know by now, that is the most powerful part of the story. Notice how the story about the burned-out family does this by describing their reactions to being presented with the check. The newspaper story could well have started with the concluding quote, but in a speech this has only one place; at the very end. The same technique was used on page 59 in the story of how my mother gave me a book of Dr. Peter Marshall's sermons, and the discovery that he often prepared his sermons around his stories just as I did. The point that both of us often used this technique could just as well have been told at the beginning. In that case, however, the suspense and curiosity you developed about why I was telling you this, and the satisfaction you felt when you finally knew my secret, would all have been lost. Take time right now to return to page 59 and experience again how that story builds to its conclusion.

Sometimes I have to tell a story to myself a total of 10 to 12 times before I achieve the dramatic effect I'm looking for. Occasionally, I can't "get it right" at all and have to let it "cool" and come back for more practice another day. But I work hard on the stories, as hard as on any part of my talks.

They give punch and credibility to the content and help produce my "big wins" with an audience. They can do the same for you.

SUMMARY OF WHAT TO KNOW AND DO

1. Remember that stories shape a speech to the habits of the mind much like a glove fits the hand.

2. Stories should usually be about oridinary people doing everyday things in extraordinary ways.

3. The tests of whether or not a story is good enough for a speech are: (1) Does it fit the life situation of the audience; will people relate to it, and (2) does it leave you pondering its meaning and significance for your own life?

4. Don't be reluctant to make some adjustments in the content of a talk in order to use a good story.

5. If an incident isn't good enough "as is," use your creative imagination to enrich it into a better one.

6. Search constantly for good stories; they are likely to turn up in family events, at work, in magazines and in other casual reading.

7. To tell powerful stories, cite the details you would notice if actually there, stick to the topic, use intimate words, talk slowly and softly and develop a surprise ending.

8. Work as hard on the stories as you do on any part of your talks.

REFERENCES

Page

70 "After gesturing for the: Haley, Alex, *Roots,* Garden City, New York: Doubleday and Co., 1976, p. 102. Copyright © 1976 by Alex Haley. Reprinted by permission of Doubleday & Company, Inc.

71 They feel as much: Tversky, Amos, and Kahneman, Daniel, "Judgment Under Uncertainty: Heuristics and Biases," *Science,* September 1974, pp. 1124-1130.

71 They look for "old: Simon, Herbert A., *Models of Thought,* New Haven: Yale University Press, 1979, pp. 386-403.

71 They need to believe: Frankl, Victor, *Man's Search for Meaning,* New York: Pocket Books, 1963.

72 High tech/high touch: From MEGATRENDS © 1982 by John Naisbitt, pp. 39 and 48. Published by Warner Books, Inc. Reprinted by permission.

73 Tversky and Kahneman term: Tversky, Amos, and Kahneman, Daniel, *op. cit.,* p. 1128.

76 Branch 6218 in Homer: *Branching Out,* Appleton, Wisconsin: Aid Association for Lutherans.

86 Psychologists refer to this: Wiener, M., and Mehrabian, A., *Language Within Language: Immediacy, A Channel In Verbal Communication,* New York: Appleton-Century Crofts, 1968, p. 31.

"People would rather dedicate their lives to a cause they believe in than lead lives of pampered idleness. The leader of a cult, a traditional religion, an army or a dynamic corporation can tap this desire."

—Dr. Warren Bemis
Professor of Management
University of Southern California

CHAPTER 4
The Secret Of Presenting Formal Lectures, Papers And Reports

When you're finished with this chapter
you will know how to design
presentations for situations in which
the basic speech is unsuitable. You
will also know how to avoid the
greatest trap in formal
presentations, which is
that they are *boring*
and get said but
not heard!

"The influence a leader exerts in altering moods, evoking images and expectations, and in establishing specific desires and objectives determines the direction a business takes. The net result of this influence is to change the way people think about what is desirable, possible and necessary."

—Abraham Zaleznik

THE SECRET OF PRESENTING FORMAL LECTURES, PAPERS AND REPORTS

FIRST OF ALL, BE CAREFUL

Almost every time you are invited to speak your survival instincts are likely to insist on a talk that is stiff, proper and formal. After all, you want to do it *right!* You're on display! You want to be accepted, to fit in with the customs and practices of the group.

Recognize that as a normal, protective reaction, and then sit yourself down and *think!* In this setting is it OK to come across as intelligent and informed, as well as human and in touch with life? Have the group's expectations and traditions been set because speakers are good, or because they are only mediocre? How would John Kennedy, Golda Meir or Martin Luther King have handled this assignment? Is there any way in the world they would have permitted themselves to be boring? Hardly! They would have been *very* informed, *very* human and *very* interesting, maybe even entertaining.

What this means for you is that, first of all, you need to be absolutely sure that the basic speech can't be made to work before you accept the formal report or lecture approach. Go back and read "How The Pattern Or System Works" on pages 57-58 again. Ask yourself how you could possibly adapt that approach to fit your situation. The fact is that very often you can.

The fact is also that sometimes you can't.

CONTROLLING IDEAS

Here are the controlling ideas for preparing and presenting papers and formal reports:

1. College professors, investment bankers and senior executives are people first. As Daniel Isenberg of Harvard Business School puts it, "managers often combine gut feel with systematic analysis, quantified data, and thoughtfulness." Keep in mind that:

   — They will have much on their minds and be tempted to take frequent side trips.

   — They may handle technical material easily, but they want it straight and to the point.

   — They will need some psychological breaks between content portions of the report.

   — They won't want to get bogged down in the muck and mire of endless details.

   — They can tell the difference between someone who understands only the subject and someone who is able to give it meaning in the larger context of life, meaning they want and need as much as anyone else.

2. Take time to clarify in your mind exactly what you are trying to accomplish through your talk. Do this in writing. If your purpose is to inform your audience, what are the major theme and subpoints you want them to learn? If you want to change the way people act or behave, what are they doing now and how do you want them to change? If you want your audience to do something, what specific actions do you want them to take? If you want to introduce yourself to a group, what do you want them to know, feel and think about you after your talk?

3. Decide very carefully whether to hand out a written report before, during or after the presentation. (If you are sincerely interested in communicating ideas and being helpful, *never* give this kind of talk without a written report to support your verbal remarks. Remember that

ear-to-brain information is limited to broad ideas and directions, and that people will keep in mind only five or six concepts or facts at a time.) If you distribute your written material before you speak, the audience will have something to see as well as hear . . . *but* they may also read ahead and not hear what you have to say. A better alternative is to distribute it at the start of your talk, but design your handout for following along and note taking. Include the additional detail that you won't cover in your talk, but organize this under short statements of your major points. Leave space for people to take notes as they use the handout to follow along in your talk. For example, if you are giving a paper on personal health and the third point is that blood cholesterol levels should be controlled, you might design that part of your handout as shown in Figure 1 on the next page. The statement of your idea is placed first and in capital letters, followed by space for note taking. Notes such as what might be taken by a listener are included in italics. Below that is added the detail that your handout provides to supplement the material presented in your verbal report. If you decide this won't work, and if you want people to listen rather than to be reading the handout, the best approach is to distribute it at the end of your talk.

4. Provide listeners with psychological breaks along the way. Do this by switching from analytical thinking based on abstract data to intuitive thinking based on illustrations and stories. Banish the notion that this is beneath the dignity of your audience. Intuitive thinking is utterly human and very much a part of the way educated and intelligent people think.

5. As much as possible skip over the technical details. Include only as many as are needed to make the major points; provide the rest in writing and for study later.

6. Assume your audience is aware and interested. They want more than generalities and polite phrases, and they won't want to be talked down to. Prepare to present your

FIGURE 1: HANDOUT DESIGN

1. CHOLESTEROL LEVELS IN THE BLOOD SHOULD BE CONTROLLED:

Reducing the levels of blood cholesterol reduces the risk of dying from coronary artery disease (CAD). Cholesterol is a white, fat-like substance made in the body for cell membranes, etc.

No matter where it comes from, once in the body cholesterol is attached to certain proteins in order to be transported through the blood stream. These micro-packages of fat (lipid) and protein, called *lipoproteins,* have been the object of intense research in the effort to uncover the link between blood cholesterol and heart disease. As it turns out, the total blood cholesterol, which is what a doctor typically measures with a blood test, reflects the amount of cholesterol contained in several different types of lipoprotein, some "good" and some "bad."

High density lipoprotein (HDL) is the good guy; it acts like a magnet to keep cholesterol from invading the inner lining of arteries. . . . The higher your level of HDL, the less likely it is that you will develop CAD. Low density lipoprotein (LDL) wears the black hat in this scenario, because it favors deposition of the cholesterol in body tissues, including artery walls. The resulting "plaques" increasingly block the channel of the artery and blood flow is diminished. . . . The higher one's level of LDL, the more likely it is that large plaques will form in the coronary arteries.

Source: Department of Continuing Education, Harvard Medical School, *Harvard Medical School Health Letter,* 79 Garden St., Cambridge, MA.

convictions and best ideas. A good way to do this is to build your talk around current controversial issues, threats or new opportunities. Controversial issues and threats often involve legislation, competition from other groups or changes in work practices. New opportunities are frequently related to emerging needs for services, changing styles and trends, and creative product developments.

7. Work at being as informal and down-to-earth as the expectations and traditions of the group will permit. Do this by the kind of stories and illustrations you select, and by the amount of time and emphasis you give them in your talk. (More time and emphasis on stories and illustrations creates more informality.) Body language can also signal informality; putting your hand in a pocket looks more casual than both hands on the podium or at your side. One trick that sometimes helps in getting away with a more relaxed approach in imposing situations is to dress very conservatively, but then speak and act more informally. The stuffed shirts who might be put off by your casual approach can at least find comfort in the fact that you know how to dress!

8. Leave time for questions at the end as a way to be both respectful and helpful.

As you think about these principles you will probably discover other ideas that will also help get your presentation heard rather than just said. That's good, because the challenge is to use everything you know to put together an appealing address that makes sense as ear-to-brain information.

WHAT IT LOOKS LIKE

The basic concept for giving a successful paper or formal report is presented in Figure 2 on the next page. As in previous drawings, the vertical line at the left indicates high and low levels of audience attention. The numbers above and below the diagram indicate time for each segment and total time elapsed. The letters ("A", "B", etc.) will be used as points of reference in the explanation.

Let's look over the major concepts first and then examine the details. First, audience energy and attention gradually decrease over time; if you talk long enough you will eventually lose *everybody*. Second, all the "bumps" are not the same size; a few are larger than others. Third, audience attention and energy recover at the conclusion and end at a high level.

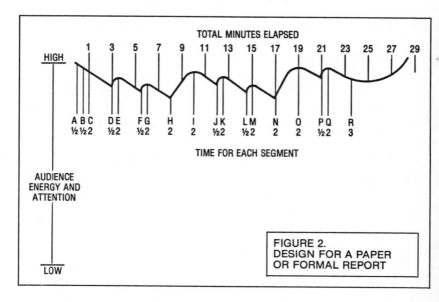

FIGURE 2.
DESIGN FOR A PAPER
OR FORMAL REPORT

POINT A

When you are introduced you will have everyone's attention out of curiosity if nothing else. Begin with some gentle affirmation of your audience by expressing appreciation for the opportunity to present your report. If the group is new to you, include a one or two sentence reference to something favorable you have heard about them or their work. If you have been with these people before, mention a common memorable experience to help cut through any lingering carry over tapes. For example: "It's good to be with you again, especially in a hotel where the restaurants serve breakfast!"

POINT B

Move directly into the statement of the major thesis of your talk. Expand on this by mentioning the supporting ideas, any additional explanation that may be helpful and the result you want to achieve. For example, "Computers can improve productivity" (major thesis). "They get work done faster and they reduce errors" (supporting ideas). "In this report I want to explain how we've used computers in my department, the good results they have produced for us and how my staff has reacted to using them" (explanation). "When I'm finished I hope you will be able to decide whether or not to investigate the possibility of computer applications in your department" (result).

POINT C

Restate your major thesis and expand on it. Keep the focus rather broad; don't overwhelm people with tedious details that can't be remembered and that slow down the flow of the more interesting major concepts.

POINT D

After about three minutes have passed, insert a 30 second change of pace into the flow of your ideas. This will reattract or refocus attention and at the same time give people a slight break from the rapid presentation of facts and information. There are several ways to do this:

1. Use a quote from a well-known sage or respected leader that illustrates your point.
2. Draw something (keep it simple and draw it BIG) on newsprint.
3. Show something on an overhead projector.

POINT E

Continue with your report. Notice that at the beginning audience attention has recovered somewhat because of the psychological break at point C, and also that it continues to drop.

POINTS F and G

At point F include the same kind of psychological break used at point D. Remember, this is only a "blip" in your presentation, not a major departure from your train of thought. At point G continue with your presentation as at point E.

POINT H

If you don't do something soon, you'll lose your audience completely! This is the time for a two minute, major psychological break which must shift your audience from an analytical, abstract line of thinking into an intuitive one. This can be done a number of ways:

1. Tell a story that illustrates one of your points. This need not be dramatic, but it must have an element of human interest.

2. Show a sample or model of the product if this would be a first-time look for most of the audience, or if your presentation is designed to help them see it in a new light. Notice that the sample or model is similar to a story in that it is concrete, and requires the audience to integrate and apply the facts and abstract ideas that you have presented up to now.

3. Have arranged with someone in the audience to make a *brief* comment that expands or explains your message. The value of this is that people receive new information, gain the perspective of another person, and hear a different voice which increases their readiness to continue listening to yours.

Continuing The Pattern

As you can see by the diagram in Figure 2, the process of alternating content with minor and major psychological breaks continues until you reach point R.

POINT R

This is where you use your *best* illustration, the one that brings meaning to your program or project by emphasizing the contribution it makes or will make to the lives of people. This need not be dramatic, but it must show in human terms why your presentation was worth time on the agenda. It should also be right to the point. For the report on how computers improved productivity, the closing story might be about someone who was helped by what the organization does. The closing comment might be, "Computers can help us do that more and better. I hope this has been helpful to you. I'll be around after the meeting if you would like to talk with me about it."

Flex The Design To Fit

There are many ways the design in Figure 2 can be adapted to fit differing audiences or situations. You might decide that the audience needs a major story or illustration earlier in the talk, and move it from point H to point F. You can vary the length of each segment slightly. You can also reduce or increase the number of segments to fit your outline. Feel free to do this, with only one caution: Try to follow the design as presented for the first presentation or two. This will give you some beginning or baseline experience. Then you will be prepared to adapt it to suit yourself and your specific situations.

How These Ideas Were Used
To Present A Major Report

A few years ago members of AAL's field management team were invited to the home office for a major training session. Their primary responsibility is to manage the marketing of insurance products that occurs through district representatives. A secondary responsibility is to manage the support the representatives provide to the leaders of AAL's local volunteer groups or "branches" — support such as program ideas, encouragement and suggestions. Help was needed with this secondary assignment because of mounting competitive pressures in the sales arena. My task was to explain how additional support for the officers of AAL's local volunteer groups or branches would be implemented and function. Previously, all help to branch leaders was provided by AAL's sales staff of district representatives. Now, volunteers, working in teams and called "Lamplighters," would work with the representatives in providing this help. The reactions to that report were very favorable, and here is how it was designed and given:

(Point A) The presentation began with an expression of appreciation for the opportunity to be on the program, and a light remark about how the Californians must be enjoying our Wisconsin snowstorm.

(Point B) I explained what conditions had created their need for the additional help, and that this presentation would inform them about a program that has been designed to meet this need.

(Point C) The name of the program (Lamplighters) was announced, and its basic purpose of providing support to the volunteer leaders was reviewed.

(Point D) The psychological break was provided with a two sentence reference to the people who had first tested the concept in Nebraska.

(Point E) An overhead projector and colored transparencies were used to explain the management responsibilities and communication links between the people involved.

(Point F) A person who had read portions of the presentation in advance had made a particularly helpful comment. It was inserted here to build support and to create a break in the flow of ideas.

(Point G) The overhead projector was used again, this time to explain the function of each paid and volunteer positon that would be involved and how it would relate to the other positions.

(Point H) Lars Granath, an AAL General Agent from Nebraska was highly respected and had provided strong support and leadership in the early years of the program. Lars gave a one and one-half minute recap of his experiences with, and conclusions about, the program.

(Points I through O) The flow continued about as you see it in Figure 2, using the overhead projector to show charts and illustrate the major points. At point N a story was used to highlight how the new approach was already working out in the field.

(Points P and Q) Questions were accepted and answered *before* telling the closing story, so that the story would provide the concluding thought.

(Point R) The final story was about a branch in Nebraska that had carried out a variety of projects which made life better for more than 20 people. This branch was brought to life through the additional information and encouragement provided by the district representative and a volunteer Lamplighter team working together. The last words were these:

"AAL branches have been doing things like this for more than 75 years. Much of what they have accomplished would not have happened without support and leadership from people like you. We're grateful for that, and we're looking forward to branches helping people even more with the additional assistance they will receive in the future. We think the volunteer Lamplighter teams will help you and will make AAL branches even better. We hope you will think so too. Thank you."

This rather formal report had only one low key "story." It was loaded with details and facts. As a banquet or luncheon speech it would have been horrible, but in this work-related setting it was well received. A good share of that was due to the way it was put together.

THE BEAUTY OF A QUOTABLE QUOTE

Quotations insert mental breaks in formal papers or lectures. They also have other attractive advantages. First, they are a good way to decorate a speech with great ideas stated memorably. That's probably what attracted you to them in the first place. Second, by adding a relevant and well chosen quotation from an outstanding leader you can add power, credibility and distinction to your message. Third, you may find quotes easier to use and deliver than stories or illustrations. This could be helpful in the early stages of your speaking career, but quotations should *not* be used as a way to avoid developing storytelling skills for basic speeches. Finally, quotes are relatively easy to find in newspapers, magazines and professional journals.

In a speech, quotes are usually introduced with transitions from the content. Here are some examples:

"This brings to mind what _____ said about our topic. In his words. . . ."

"_____ commented on just this problem when she said. . . ."

"This is not a new situation. Even _____ commented on it. He said. . . ."

Finally

Remember that formal lectures or papers are automatically less interesting and appealing to most people than the basic speech presented in chapter three. However, if you design them according to Figure 2, your presentation stands a very good chance of being better than those presented by 90 percent of the people you know.

SUMMARY OF ACTIONS TO TAKE

1. Be absolutely sure that the basic speech can't be made to work before you accept the formal report or lecture approach.

2. Take time to clarify in your mind exactly what you are trying to accomplish through your talk. Do this in writing.

3. Decide very carefully whether to hand out a written report before, during or after the presentation.

4. Provide listeners with psychological breaks along the way. Do this by switching from analytical thinking based on abstract data to intuitive thinking based on illustrations and stories.

5. As much as possible skip over the technical details.

6. Assume your audience is aware and interested; provide more than generalities and polite phrases. Prepare to share your best ideas and convictions with them.

7. Work at being as informal and down-to-earth as the expectations and traditions of the group will permit.

8. Leave time for questions at the end.

9. Consider using a quotation in place of a story or illustration.

REFERENCES

Page

92 "The influence a leader: Zaleznik, Abraham, "Managers and Leaders: Are They Different?" *Harvard Business Review,* May-June 1977, p. 71.

94 As Daniel Isenberg of: Isenberg, Daniel J., "How Senior Managers Think," *Harvard Business Review,* November-December 1984, p. 86.

94 Remember that ear-to: Simon, Herbert A., *Models of Thought,* New Haven: Yale University Press, 1979, p. 52.

"Luck is what happens when
preparation meets opportunity."

—Elmer Letterman

CHAPTER 5
The Secret Of
Advance Questions**

If you know what questions to ask at
the very beginning, you can save
yourself hours of work and a lot of
frustration and grief. You can also
avoid dumb mistakes and put
yourself on the road to a very
successful speech. After reading
this chapter you will know
what questions to ask, why
they are important and how
to ask them.

**This chapter has been saved until now, because it
makes more sense after you understand audience behavior
and how to design a speech.

"Shallow men believe in luck."

—Emerson

THE SECRET OF ADVANCE QUESTIONS

ADVANCE QUESTIONS BRING
IMPORTANT BENEFITS

Immediately after accepting a speaking invitation you need to gather essential information by asking several pointed questions. What you do and what you learn will greatly increase your chances for success. Here's why:

1. You need to know some things about the people in your audience in order to prepare a speech that is tailored to them. You need to know about their biases and peculiarities, their expectations of you, and whether you will be a welcome or an unwanted guest.

2. The information you gather will reduce your level of uncertainty and frustration. There is no more graphic illustration of this than those Londoners during World War II who actually were relieved when the bombs began falling each night. Just knowing makes one feel better.

3. Thoughtful questions, more than declarations or silence, communicate that you are serious about doing a good job, interested in being helpful and know what you are doing.

4. Questions are a subtle and socially acceptable way to communicate a positive self-definition for yourself; they send messages about what you expect, and that you don't want to be taken for granted. As Russell Jones says in his helpful and thought-provoking book, *Self-Fulfilling Prophecies:*

". . . impressions and situations are "managed" for a purpose, and the techniques people employ in their attempts at impression management are simply techniques for communicating expectancies, expectations about how they are to be treated and how they intend to treat others."

Two major barriers will hinder you from asking the right questions in the right way. One is the tendency to be so pleased about being asked to speak that you forget all about them. If that happens, make another contact and collect the necessary information. Any uncomfortable feelings you experience will pay off in a better speech and help you remember next time to ask your questions immediately. The other is our tendency to be reluctant about "bothering" someone with our detailed concerns and questions. Put reluctance aside with the realization that you can't be a helpful person if you don't know what's needed. Remember that you will be on public display and can't afford to take chances with your reputation. Assume the attitude that if an occasion is important enough for someone to ask you to give even a five minute speech, then it's important enough for you to ask a few questions that will help you do a good job.

Use Your Judgment

For any speech of five minutes and more, you need answers to all the following questions before preparation work begins. This doesn't mean you need to ask every question in this chapter, since in most cases you will know the answers to many of them from your prior contact and experience. Also, of course, you can be satisfied with less complete information for a five minute talk than if you are to give the major address of 20 minutes or more. Use your judgment; avoid anything like the ridiculous extreme of taking 20 minutes to ask 10 detailed questions for two minutes of "remarks or greetings." Remember, however, that you cannot give a successful talk if you do not have adequate answers to all the questions in this chapter.

Help The Other Person Respond

It will be easier to ask questions and get helpful answers if the person asking you to speak is in the proper frame of mind. Chances are that he or she is not an experienced speaker, and as a result may be nervous about asking you to prepare and give a talk. After you have been asked to give a speech, say yes, and take care of any adjustments you want to make in the topic (covered in chapter six). Then help create the proper mental framework this way: Say something like, "I need your answers to a few questions that will help me do what you want." Continue with any or all of the following that you need to ask.

QUESTIONS THAT HELP OTHERS

Asking all necessary questions in this category first communicates your primary interest in being helpful and doing a good job (rather than simply taking care of old number one). It also lets the other person know that you are willing to share control of the situation. Shared control makes it easier for the person extending the invitation to conclude later that you did a good job. This is demonstrated by an area of psychology called "illusion of control." People who are allowed to choose one of four unmarked cans of soda like their first choice better than people who are only allowed to choose from one of two unmarked cans. The drinks are the same in all cans, but thinking that we have more control helps us feel better about what we choose.

1. *Tell me about the audience: Size? Mostly men or women? Common characteristics? Expectations they'll have for my talk?*

2. *Tell me about how they will view my talk: Expectations? Accepting of, or resistant to, my topic? Will I be a welcome or an unwanted guest?*

This information is especially important if you will be speaking to an unknown group. While unnecessary for understanding how an audience will reason or "think" (they all do it the same), you must design a speech that gains their acceptance and trust, and that gets your point across. Recently, I neglected to pin this down, and my stories and illustrations, planned for young mothers, fell flat when the actual audience turned out to be a group of 65- to 75-year-old grandmothers! It was a dumb mistake. The result was a very average talk; not a failure but far from my best. The rule is: Find out to whom you will be speaking. Know your audience.

3.   *How long should I plan to speak?*

This may not seem important at the time, but you will be very concerned about it once the program begins. Speakers are often asked to shorten their talks at the last minute, simply because they failed to establish a clear contract for time when they were first asked to speak. And you *need* that contract because

— you can't be helpful if you give only half a talk,
— you will be investing hours in preparation, and you won't want them to be wasted,
— your reputation is on the line!

Therefore, always ask pointedly about this, and be persistent until you receive a specific answer. Usually the person will respond with an approximation ("about 20 minutes"), or a range ("five to seven minutes"). Then repeat the answer immediately ("OK, I'll prepare for five to seven minutes.") as a clear signal that you are serious about the time limit, and that you also expect others to be. Repeat it again in a closing summary statement at the end of the conversation. Say something like, "Thanks for asking me to speak. The things you've said give me a good idea about what you want. I'll give a five to seven minute report on the new machine in my area at your next staff meeting." If the person extending the invitation has a reputation for being disorganized or cutting speakers short, you might want to follow the conversation with a brief note that confirms the topic and the time allocation. Adding a sentence expressing appreciation for the opportunity to speak will put a "smile on your nudge" and help maintain a positive relationship.

Despite all this, there is always the possibility that at the last minute you will have no choice but to shorten your talk anyway. How to prepare and do this is covered in chapter seven.

4. *After I finish my talk, what should the audience know, feel and/or do?*

This is the "million dollar" question that probes beneath the topic on which you've been asked to speak and reveals what your talk is *really* supposed to accomplish. Often those extending the invitation have not organized their thoughts about what they actually want from you. This question helps them do that, and surfaces all kinds of hidden or even conflicting hopes and agendas. For the time invested it does more to produce winning speeches than anything else. Use the answer to give people what they want, rather than what you want, and you will come off a consistent winner.

I never agree to give an important speech without asking this question just the way it is written above, and for a major address I ask the person to give me a written response in a letter or memo. Asking it has also enabled me to avoid situations where I was asked to be a miracle worker ("I need you to restore the morale of my staff."), or where I could have been manipulated for someone's advantage. While such traps are rare, doing some deft footwork around them is better than being drawn into a mess.

QUESTIONS THAT HELP YOURSELF

Try to ask these questions after you have demonstrated primary interest in giving a helpful speech. They may be "cushioned" with a comment like, "Now I hope you can help me with a few details that will be very important on the day I give the talk."

5. *Where will I be speaking? How do I get there? Where can I park my car?*

I can still feel the tension welling up inside as Audrey and I raced down strange roads in our red and white 1955 Oldsmobile. Usually we had only a few minutes left to find the places at which I was to speak. Often Audrey held tiny slips of paper under the glove compartment light trying to make sense out of the three or four words I had scribbled as directions. This was no fun, and the speeches I gave weren't either. Write down the exact name of the church, business, restaurant or whatever, the exact address information and good directions about how to get there. If you remember the question about parking, you might get a good spot right next to the door, instead of a long walk in the rain.

6.   *Where will I be speaking in the program?*

As you will recall from chapter one (page 29), the position of your talk in the total program is important. This question is included here so that you can use this list as a future reference. Remember that it's important to determine your program position; request a change if you are giving a major talk and it seems necessary.

7.   *Will there be a podium and a microphone?*

Speakers who fail to inquire about these are simply foolish; they are the last things you need to be wondering about. If you want a podium and none is at hand, ask for one. If you think you need a microphone and none is available, request one. Don't be bashful about this, and don't hold back in an effort to be "nice." Nice doesn't count for much after doing a lousy job. The nicest thing you can do is to secure what you need to do your best. Consider also that you're going to make a special effort for the talk, and you have a right to expect others to do likewise. Go so far as saying you will bring your own podium if none can be found and you need one to feel comfortable. If you begin to speak often you may even decide to obtain your own microphone and avoid the cheap imitations you're likely to find even in expensive hotels. I have one with a set of adapters that enables me to plug into almost any kind of sound system. It's been a lifesaver many times.

8.   *Will water be available where I speak?*

This may be unnecessary for you, especially for a speech of 10 minutes or less. You'll know after giving one or two.

9. *What clothing is appropriate?*

While we live in a time where "anything goes" concerning clothes, you generally want to be dressed like the leadership of your audience. A sport shirt and slacks still look out of place in a room full of conservative suits and dresses. Even more important, audience attention is distracted by inappropriate clothing that gets in the way of the message you want to communicate and the impression you want to make. Studies by Dion and others demonstrate that people expect attractive persons to have better jobs and more success than unattractive ones. Select and use clothes so that you can forget them and give full attention to your talk.

A good practice for both men and women is to wear a well-pressed suit. If you find when you arrive that the atmosphere is more casual, coat and even tie can be easily removed as a friendly signal that you want to be part of the group.

10. *Can or should I bring my spouse or a friend?*

Being clear about this avoids uncertainty and surprises for everyone. Let's face it, having your spouse at an extra chair on the end of a head table with nothing to eat *is* a little awkward. Or, when everyone expected you to bring your spouse, a solo appearance is rather lonely. Ask, and the answer will put another worry to rest.

SUMMARY OF ACTIONS TO TAKE

Make sure you know how to answer all of the following questions before beginning to prepare a talk. Ask only as many as necessary.

Ask these questions first:

1. Tell me about the audience: Size? Mostly men or women? Common characteristics? Special biases? Peculiarities? Etc.
2. Tell me about how they will view my talk? Expec-

tations? Accepting of, or resistant to, my topic? Will I be a welcome or an unwanted guest?

3. How long should I plan to speak?

4. After I finish my talk, what should the people in the audience know, feel and/or do?

Ask these questions second:

5. Where will I be speaking? How do I get there? Where can I park my car?

6. Where will I be speaking in the program?

7. Will there be a podium and a microphone?

8. Will water be available where I speak?

9. What clothing is appropriate?

10. Can or should I bring my spouse or a friend?

REFERENCES

109 There is no more graphic: Janis, I. L., *Air War and Emotional Stress,* New York: McGraw Hill, 1951.

109 As Russell Jones says: Jones, Russell A., *Self-Fulfilling Prophecies,* Hillsdale, New Jersey: Lawrence Erlbaum Associates, 1977, p. 117.

111 People who are allowed: Salancik, Gerald R., "Commitment and the Control of Organizational Behavior and Belief," *New Directions In Organizational Behavior,* Chicago: St. Clair Press, pp. 20ff.

115 Studies by Dion and: Dion, K., Berscheid, E., and Walster, E., "What Is Beautiful Is Good," *Journal of Personality and Social Psychology,* 1965, pp. 434 - 440.

CHAPTER 6
The Secret Of Research And Writing

This secret is not the fact that you must do these things; it is how to do them right. "Right" begins with an efficient way to research a topic. It continues with knowing how to let the speech almost write itself, as well as how to prepare notes for use at the podium. When you are finished with this chapter you will know exactly how to go about each of these . . . and why!

"It is continual diligence, effort and commitment on a regular basis, that makes things happen."

—John Naber
USA Winner of Four Gold Medals
in the 1976 Olympics

THE SECRET OF RESEARCH AND WRITING

HOW TO DO RESEARCH FOR A SPEECH

Research and writing are trade secrets because they involve much more than the iron-willed application of time and energy. What follows is the step-by-step research process for preparing a speech.

1. The Rule Of Half And Half

Your initial task is NOT to gather great quantities of magazines, newspapers and books for background reading and fact finding. What almost everybody fails to recognize is that in preparing a talk, the proportion of research and writing to practice is roughly half and half. Most speakers do quite the opposite. If they invest 10 hours in preparing a presentation, five hours go into the research phase, four into writing and one into some sort of mental review that they think is "practice." If *you* choose to invest 10 hours in preparing a talk, you must spend no more than two hours in reading and research, no more than three hours in writing, and at least five hours in directed practice.

Why the limited time for research? Remember that a speech must be limited to presenting a few, simple, large and dynamic ideas. Extensive reading and research piles up more information than you can possibly use in a 20 minute talk, and only adds time and frustration to the process of boiling it all down again to what you really have time to say.

Why the limited time for writing? Because what you write must be changed, shaped and polished into your speaking style and language. This takes time, and without enough of it your practice can focus on nothing more than learning to *read* your manuscript. That kind of "speech" is given by most of the people you know, which is why you can learn to be better than 90 percent of them.

2. How To Avoid Wasting Many Hours On Needless Research

First of all, it simply makes good sense to accept only those speaking topics about which you can give a decent speech without doing any research at all. Speak about what you know! If a topic is suggested about which you are uninformed, propose an alternate one. You may be surprised at how easily a topic can usually be changed, often because the requester sees you as doing a kind deed or favor. Let's say, by way of illustration, that someone called and asked you to speak at Joe's retirement party, and to talk about the many things Joe has done for the organization over the years. Since you want to be helpful and value every opportunity to speak, you agree willingly. However, this particular topic would require you to look up Joe's personnel records, and talk with many of his former bosses and associates. You correctly conclude this would be a waste of time. You now have three choices:

A. Suggest an alternative immediately

If you can suggest an alternate topic immediately, say something like, "Sure, I'll be glad to speak. However, I think a slightly different approach would be better for me. Would it be okay if I made a few brief references to Joe's work during his years with the organization, and focused more on what he has done while working in my area? With the time I have available to do research, I'm sure I can do a better job with this approach."

B. Ask for time to think about the topic

If you have no immediate alternative, say something like, "Yes, I'll be glad to speak, but I would like to call you back in a day or two, after I have had time to think about your topic suggestion. I may want to propose something slightly different if what you've suggested doesn't seem just right for me." Then call back within two days and recommend a topic that is better for you.

C. Accept and adapt

This approach is the boldest and often the best. Assume that the person asking you has only a general notion of what is wanted, and that anything close, if well done, will be fine. Say something like, "Sure, I'll be glad to develop something along the general lines you suggest." Then proceed on your assumption; develop a talk around the *general* topic suggested, but very much as you want. Chances are, no one will ever know the difference, and even if they do they probably won't care.

If you value time, you will work diligently to adjust speech topics into your information-rich areas for all but the most stringent work related assignments. It is simply inexcusable to be pouring over source materials for hours on end to research a topic someone just happened to suggest.

3. Facts And Figures Are Essential

A speech must communicate information, and the ideas you present must be carefully supported with facts and figures that add depth and substance. If you are speaking on a subject you already know rather well, you will need only to read a few book chapters or magazine articles to gather more than enough factual information. The ever-present temptation is to say more than time permits, and more than an audience can grasp. GIVE IN AND YOU WILL RUIN YOUR CHANCES FOR SUCCESS! Two or three facts and/or figures in each content section is usually about right. A good way to select these is to concentrate on identifying those related to your topic's major concepts and trends, and to ignore those related to details.

Occasionally you may be asked to speak on a subject about which you know relatively little. If so, don't feel you need to have read everything in order to prepare adequately. Review several good books or articles, pick out what seems reasonable and fitting and call it good enough. If you spend a limited amount of time well, you will almost certainly find more than enough valuable information for a short talk. If someone does challenge your facts, give your sources confidently and ask them if they have others to suggest.

The Library

Libraries have bad reputations in many of our minds, possibly because of unpleasant childhood experiences, or because they are unfamiliar. In our information age, however, they are an open door to a better future. If the public library is not yet one of your familiar resources, determine now to make it one. You will be amazed at what you will find; friendly people who sincerely want to help, *organized* information (more than you'd ever imagine) so that you can find what you want on almost any subject, a quiet place to work, and practically no charges! If you can read this book, you can quickly learn how to use the card catalog to find books on your topic. The librarian will help you. He or she will also show you how to use the *Reader's Guide To Periodical Literature* (no more of a mystery than the card catalog) to locate the magazine articles you need. Up-to-date encyclopedias are waiting to be used. And if you need something the library doesn't have, it can be borrowed from another one nearby, usually for a small charge.

There is a difference between the kinds of books and magazines you will find in a public library and those available at a college or university. Ask at your public library about the location of college or university libraries in your area and how you may use them. Then give yourself another treat and poke around there for a few hours to get an idea of the scholarly journals and references available. It will be worth every minute of your time and much more.

HOW TO WRITE A SPEECH

Along life's way adults are expected to have learned many things which are far from common knowledge . . . like how to

—manage money
—stay healthy
—raise children
—write a speech.

While it is considered impolite to ask someone if they know how to do any of these, few people actually know how to do even most of them really well. To provide you with whatever help may be necessary, we will actually "write" the speech on drug abuse that was outlined previously. As you know, its earlier purpose was to illustrate the process of searching for stories. You can review it by turning to pages 77-81.

Gather Information

The first step in writing a speech is to gather the information you need. Begin by reading through whatever materials on the topic you may have at hand. If this happens to be a stack of "stuff" two feet high, quickly sort through it and pick out the best half dozen items and read those.

Take notes as you go; make it a point to write only one idea on each piece of paper. This will usually be one to three sentences, no more than a paragraph or two at most. If you want to save paper, cut 8½" by 11" pages to 5½" by 8½". Here are quotes from an article that you might write on two separate sheets:

"Rep. Lester Wolff (D.,N.Y.), . . . said: 'The United States is the most pervasive drug-abusing nation in history. And our most pervasive illegal drug of abuse is marijuana. . . . Wolff noted that one in nine high school seniors was smoking pot on a daily or near-daily basis . . . that pot smoking is now common among junior high students; that evidence indicates pot smoking among 8- to 12-year-olds is increasing.'"

Mann, Peggy, "Marijuana Alert," *Reader's Digest,* December 1979, pp. 139 and 140.

"Dr. Robert Heath, chairman of the Department of Neurology and Psychiatry at Tulane Medical School: 'It would seem from . . . studies that you have to use marijuana for only a relatively short time in moderate to heavy use before evidence of brain damage begins to develop.' ''

Mann, Peggy, "Marijuana Alert," *Reader's Digest,* December 1979, p. 141.

Don't try to organize your information yet; just write down one idea per sheet and add source references in case you want to check something again later. If stories or illustrations of various points come to mind, write a brief note about each of them too, again one to a sheet. After you've done this it will be time to spend an hour or two in the library checking recent books and articles to make sure your facts are up to date. Again, write every item of information on a separate sheet. Remember not to overdo this research; stop collecting information when you have enough to give a good talk, and before you have become the world's expert on all the finer details of your topic!

Organize Your Material

Find a place where you can spread out all your notes and organize them into piles. A large table or the living room floor usually works well. Look over your notes and figure out what seems to go together. For the speech on drug abuse you might find that you have some items about the nature and extent of the problem, some about what police and others are doing to fight it, some about what parents can do to help their children with this threat, some stories and illustrations and some left over pieces that don't seem to fit anywhere.

Now, gather all the notes that relate to a particular part of your topic and place them in a small pile. This might be from one to six pieces of paper. When this is done you will probably have four or five piles of usable material, and another pile of leftovers. Next, take the pile that relates to the first supporting point in your talk. In the case of the drug abuse speech this would be the pile on the nature and extent of the problem; what you will use for your first supporting idea, or point D on page 81. (The same final speech outline appears again on page 126.) Arrange the notes in this pile in logical order and as you want to talk about them. For example, be sure that you introduce a subject before presenting the details about it. Do this with each pile, except the one containing the stories and illustrations, and put a paper clip on the pages in each pile.

Then, arrange the paper-clipped piles in the order they will be used in your speech, and insert the sheets about the stories and illustrations where you plan to use them. The complete stack of materials for the drug abuse speech would now contain the following:

1. A single sheet about the opening story (point C, major thesis).

2. A pile of sheets about the extent and nature of the problem (point D, first supporting idea).

3. A single sheet about the story of the police chief from another town (point F).

4 A pile of sheets about police efforts and the need for support (point G, second supporting idea).

5. The sheets containing notes from phone calls to the police chief and the superintendent of schools (point I).

6. A pile of sheets about what parents can do to help their children (point J, third supporting idea).

7. A single sheet about the concluding story (point L).

Select The Best Place And Time

The best place to write is a quiet spot where you won't be disturbed for several hours. The best *time* to write is at least two days after you have completed your research and have decided on your outline and stories. This will give your subconscious mind time to process the data and make conceptual connections. During the two days you will notice ideas and word combinations "sparking" into your mind; these will ignite your thought processes as you begin to write.

It's also best not to delay too long. Rushing to complete your preparations in the last few days and hours produces stress, and stress decreases one's ability to learn. Occasionally you will have to try writing more than once, so give yourself enough time for a few false starts and mistakes. The key is to organize your time so that you can write in a relaxed frame of mind and with plenty of time remaining for other preparation activities.

Visualize

Sit down to write and begin by opening this book to the figure in chapter two or four that designs the particular speech you are planning to give. Study this so that you are familiar with how the content and stories flow through the talk. Then read through your outline; the one for the speech on drugs finally developed into this:

Point C: Major thesis: Drug pushers must be stopped!

Point C: Story: Kids getting drugs at school.

Point D: First supporting idea: The nature and extent of the problem.

Point F: Story: Police chief from another town.

Point G: Second supporting idea: Police departments need our support!

Point I: Story: Phone calls to police chief and superintendent of schools.

Point J: Third supporting idea: Family discussions about drugs are essential!

Point L: Story for conclusion: Boy devastated by pushers.

Next, visualize the speaking situation in detail, and imagine yourself behaving in the strong confident way you desire. Hold that image in your mind for several breaths, and feel the respect and approval coming from the audience and right to you. (If you are not familiar with this technique or question its value, it may be helpful to read about it in *Psycho-Cybernetics* by Dr. Maxwell Maltz.)

Then, take the top sheet in the stack of paper you have prepared and write or type words about that exactly as you might say them. In general you can use material right off your notes, only adding connecting ideas and putting it more into your own words so that you will feel comfortable saying it. You will find that by using the prepared pieces of paper in this way the speech will almost "write itself"; all you will have to do is change it into your own words and add connecting thoughts to link one idea to the next. Try to write as you talk; use small words rather than large ones; keep the sentences short. If the person who will introduce you is named Bruce, you might start this way:

DRUG PUSHERS MUST BE STOPPED
Service Club Speech
Date

Introduction

Thanks, Bruce, for that kind introduction. As all of you know, it's better than I deserve, but who am I to complain. When I was asked to speak to your club today, I felt honored and pleased because I admire what you have done for this community, and because I care very much about today's topic. (Notice that this is a transition into what comes next.)

Since our subject today is on drug problems, let's see what common experiences and information we share. (Remember, you could ask questions that would reveal how *little* your listeners know, and thereby turn them off. What you want to do is silence their carry over tapes, gain trust and help them open their minds.)

First of all, how many of us grew up in an environment that, for all practical purposes, was free of marijuana, heroin and cocaine? (Pause for a show of hands.) *OK. That was true for me too. I really wasn't confronted with these drugs in elementary and high school when I was growing up.*

Another question, how many of us even today feel that when it comes right down to it, we know relatively little about drugs? (Pause for a show of hands.) *OK. That was also true of me until recently. I just had no particular reason to find out about this, so I used my time for other things and didn't bother.*

One more: How many of us have at least a vague notion that the temptations our kids face may well be serious, and that pos-

sibly we should be very concerned? (Pause for a show of hands.) *Fine! That was also true of me, but I never really knew what to do about it. Today I'm concerned as a parent, not because I think my two boys are on drugs, but because I love them just as all of us who are parents love our kids.*

Drug Pushers Must Be Stopped!
(Story and major thesis)

I'm pleased to learn from your answers to these questions that I'm very much like you. It makes me feel right at home . . . like I'm talking to friends. As you may know, I've been looking into the problem of kids and drugs for about a year and a half now, and I've learned much about a very serious problem.

To show you what I've learned, I'd like you to come with me to Long Island, New York — to the suburban town of Beth-page. I want you to meet Joan and Doug Benning and their son, Peter. Peter is a nice kid, a ninth grader with red hair and freckles on his nose.

Tell story. (Notice that you don't write out the story, just the beginning and ending statements that you want to say perfectly.)

Story ending: After they found Peter's body, Joan and Doug went to the hospital to identify it. Coming from that horrible room, stunned and confused beyond words, they met their pastor and a detective. Putting his arms around them both, the pastor led them in a prayer for faith, peace and strength. Then he said, "They found two things in Peter's pockets. One was a syringe. Another was this note." In their son's handwriting it said, "Mom and Dad — I love you. Peter."

Friends, drug pushers must be stopped! They are a stinking sickness in our towns and homes, and they simply must be stopped! (Now comes the transition into the first content section.) *If Peter Benning was an isolated case it would be tragic enough, but he was part of a group of victimized children, part of a national tragedy involving millions of young people and billions of dollars each year.*

The National Tragedy

(First Supporting Idea)

Listen to Representative Lester Wolff of New York, Chairman of the House of Representatives Select Committee on Narcotics Abuse and Control. "The United States is the most pervasive drug-abusing nation in history. And our most pervasive illegal drug of abuse is marijuana." Wolff also reported

— *that one in nine high school seniors was smoking pot on a daily or near-daily basis, an almost 80 percent increase in three years' time*
— *that pot smoking is now common among junior high students*
— *that evidence indicates pot smoking among eight- to 12-year-olds is increasing.*

Contrary to what you may have heard, smoking pot is harmful to the body. Here's Dr. Robert Heath, chairman of the Department of Neurology and Psychiatry at Tulane Medical School: "It would seem from (clinical) studies that you have to use marijuana for only a relatively short time in moderate to heavy use before evidence of brain damage begins to develop.

And here's Dr. Gabriel Nahas of Columbia University, College of Physicians and Surgeons, who discovered that exposure to marijuana diminished the capacity of individual cells to orchestrate life: "Today's pot smoker may not only be damaging his own mind and body, but may be playing genetic roulette and casting a shadow across children and grandchildren yet unborn."

(Transition and Second supporting idea)

These national leaders aren't the only ones who are concerned; it extends right down to the local level too. I want you to meet Bill Veno, Chief of Police in Marysville, Ohio. (Now move into your second story, writing only the beginning and ending sentences of what you want to say.)

Continue writing in this way until your talk is complete. The final words you write should be the last few sentences of your concluding story, followed by a short restatement of your major idea, then ending with the words, "Thank you."

SUMMARY OF ACTIONS TO TAKE

1. Spend half of your preparation time on research and writing, the other half on actual practice.

2. Accept only those speaking topics about which you can give a fairly good speech without doing any research at all.

3. If a topic is suggested about which you are uninformed, arrange for one you can give without doing extensive research.

4. If you aren't already, become familiar with your public library and how to use it.

5. Take notes on what you read about your topic. Put only one idea or one story on a single piece of paper. Place all the sheets relating to each part of your talk into a group, one group for each part. Arrange the groups, and the individual sheets in each group, in the order you want to talk about them.

6. Do your writing in a place where you won't be disturbed and at least two days after you have completed your research.

7. Start with the top piece of paper and let the speech "write itself" from the notes you've taken. Merely add connecting ideas and put everything in your own words.

Page
126 (If you are not: Maltz, Maxwell, *Psycho-Cybernetics,* N. Hollywood, California: Wilshire Book Co., 1977, pp. 27-43.

CHAPTER 7
The Secret Of Enlightened Practice

Enlightened practice has the power to change ordinary people into outstanding speakers. It has mystery about it, and it can produce magical results for you. This chapter tells you how to do it, why it works and why people admire those who use it well.

"You can map out a fight plan or a life plan. But when the action starts you're down to your reflexes. That's where your roadwork shows. If you cheated on that in the dark of the morning, you're getting found out now under the bright lights."

—Joe Frazier

THE SECRET OF ENLIGHTENED PRACTICE

This is a valued and reliable "old friend." It is a treasure that has mystery in it; a habit as familiar as house slippers; and something I trust because it has never failed to produce good results. It is also the good news, bad news secret, and both are very important.

The good news is this: USING WHAT YOU WILL LEARN HERE, YOU CAN BECOME A POWERFUL SPEAKER THROUGH PRACTICE. You don't have to be born with speaking talent, lucky, rich enough for expensive lessons, incredibly smart or anything else. The only thing you need is to release desire and determination in the form of enlightened practice. To listeners who do not know this, the results will seem like magic. Their eyes and common senses will tell them you are indeed a natural leader or born speaker, and your capacity to be helpful to other people and to an organization will be substantially increased.

The bad news is this: PRACTICE IS THE ONLY WAY TO SUCCESS. Expensive lessons, talent, luck and brains will not do it. Time, effort, persistence and determination are essential, and those who lack or neglect to develop these simple virtues will not be able to blame failure on anything else.

What Enlightened Practice
Can Do For You

A few years ago I was invited to a White House luncheon hosted by President Reagan as part of his program to increase volunteering and philanthropy. National leaders of a wide variety of non-profit organizations were present, and I was attending both as a staff member of AAL and a member of the board of directors of VOLUNTEER: The National Center. I had just checked into the hotel when Kenn Allen, VOLUN-TEER'S president on loan to the White House for Reagan's project, telephoned: "Would you give a four minute speech at the luncheon about AAL's volunteer programs and its plans for the future?"

Speaking on this occasion was totally unexpected, but I thanked Kenn for the invitation and said yes. There was exactly one hour and forty-five minutes left to prepare, and I used it all, first to write out my talk, and then literally to polish it to a razor's edge.

Several hundred chairs had been set up in the East Room, and they were all filled. The anticipation and excitement in the air increased even more with the powerful and familiar announcement from the back of the room: "Ladies and gentlemen, the President of the United States!" He came through the big, polished doors with a smile and a wave, surrounded by a Secret Service cadre of seven unsmiling men and one woman, who marched in smartly and took their sentry-like places around the room. Klieg lights blazed and cameras clicked and rolled while Reagan approached the podium to a standing ovation. A photographer, kneeling on the floor off to his left, took four or five pictures under the unblinking stare of a no-nonsense Secret Service agent. The President spoke for a few minutes, excused himself and left with the same smiles and fanfare that marked his entry.

The program continued under the capable leadership of Mrs. Elizabeth Dole, and soon it was announced that persons from five organizations would speak briefly to the group. Speakers one and two were introduced, talked briefly and received what amounted to polite and somewhat perfunctory applause, followed by a "thank you" from Mrs. Dole. The third speaker was a woman who, like all of us, was asked to speak for four minutes. She did it in nine, even presenting a book to the chairperson in recognition of something the audience never understood. When she sat down we could just feel everyone in the room heave a grateful sigh of relief.

My introduction came next. I said thanks for the opportunity to share AAL's story, described a local branch in three sentences, and reported that AAL had 5500 of them and was adding more each year. I described a project one branch was having that evening for a family with severe health problems, and ended with this:

Madam Chairman: Aid Association for Lutherans has a deep and enduring commitment to volunteering as a fundamental part of our democracy. We see it as a way to make a difference in the lives of people and to make our nation better tomorrow than it is today. We will continue and we will expand our commitment to volunteering. We hope others will join us in developing this vital part of our free society. Thank you very much."

The applause, stronger than "polite," told part of the story. Another part was told through the words of Mrs. Dole who expressed thanks "for that powerful statement" and in a tone that said she meant it. And the many people who thanked me personally after the meeting told the rest. It *was* a good three minute talk. It had a powerful impact. It had been heard rather than only said. Why? Not because I was smarter or had a better topic.

The difference was very clear: *Enlightened Practice!* A familiar and trusted "old friend" helped me know exactly how to use that one hour and forty-five minutes. There was a pattern to follow, a way that had been traveled before. After you practice a few talks this way, my old friend will be your friend too. But there are no shortcuts. Our talks will be only as good as we prepare them to be.

WHY PRACTICE WILL PRODUCE ALMOST MAGICAL RESULTS FOR YOU

Psychologists Tversky and Kahneman gave subjects skimpy, unreliable information about an individual and then asked them to guess the person's occupation. For example, they might say that Sue is 30-years-old, quiet, successful in her field, not involved in social or political issues, tidy, likes to read and is well-liked by her friends. Then they would ask subjects whether Sue is an engineer or a librarian. People expressed great confidence that Sue was a librarian, even though this conclusion could not be justified on the basis of the information they were given. They used their "patterns" or their stereotypes in coming to the conclusion that Sue was not an engineer.

And that's all they could do! The world's leading cognitive psychologists take great pains to emphasize that it is simply impossible to consider all the data all the time and make completely rational decisions. Simon says that people must be content, "to find 'good enough' solutions to their problems and 'good enough' courses of action." Secord relates this to the problem all of us have in sizing up another person:

> "Certainly it is not feasible to observe and grasp each individual in all his uniqueness and still carry on the smooth, fast-moving interaction with other persons which is characteristic of most everyday relationships. A reasonable assumption is that each perceiver has a set of person categories (of which stereotypes are the most obvious) into which he classifies those with whom he interacts."

Also, remember what Festinger found: We evaluate people, not objectively against a set standard, but subjectively in relation to ourselves and others in the group.

The inescapable conclusion is that when you speak, especially in platform situations, the table is set for others to collect important personal information. What they understand about you may well multiply many times in a matter of minutes. Often the audience will include people who will make the critical decisions affecting your future. If you come across as informed, confident, logical, positive and inspiring, they will "fill in the blanks" and perceive you as having a multitude of equally desirable qualities. If you come across as confused, unsure, searching, narrow and weak, they will see you in an entirely different light. Sensing this, most people avoid up-front presentations like the plague and choose to display only wallflower silence.

As a result, they deny themselves the opportunity to show others their talent and potential, and do not make their full contributions as effective, helping persons. Interestingly, low profile silence does not bring the protection and security that people hope will accompany it. Even the wallflower is judged, and often harshly. What choice do any of us have but to "get out there" and do our best with what we have or can learn? The answer, of course, is none.

This way of forming opinions of people may seem very superficial and unfair. But we use exactly this approach in making our evaluations of others. As you know.

The nice thing about it, however, is that all you need do is prepare to the point of being able to speak better than nine out of 10 people in your group or organization, and folks will begin to imagine all sorts of good things about you. If you want to check this out, think over your own reactions to someone who can stand up, and with seeming ease, deliver a polished and powerful speech. You don't merely comment on his or her speaking ability; you also remark about confidence, flair, intelligence, talent, etc. You *assume* that what you saw happened because of the kind of person you perceive him or her to be. It never crosses your mind that what you saw might actually be a skilled "performance" resulting from enlightened preparation.

If the impression thus created is merely an illusion of competence over what in reality is ignorance or deceit, it will work only briefly if at all. Most of us cannot fool *any* of the people *any* of the time, and even trying it would make us feel cheap and phony. Unfortunately, the plague of the majority is that diligence, competence and know-how are savagely masked by poor speaking skills. However, when enlightened practice brings out the talents and true qualities of their real selves, the effect is as appealing and wholesome as a rainbow after a summer rain.

What you become through preparation is honestly and legitimately yours to claim and use. With repeated preparation the old "you" will simply cease to exist and be forgotten, and a new and more effective person will come to live in its place.

There is no better proof of this than Sir Winston Churchill. In his early years Churchill's addresses were heavy and cumbersome, but he developed himself into the best speaker of his time. Much of this was due to his practice of working hard and long over what he wanted to say. Jack Valenti says this of him: "Sir Winston, arguably the finest orator of his generation, always wrote out what he wanted to say, then transferred the written text to notes which he scrawled in his own hand or had typed after he had polished them to his satisfaction. This was his unvarying method of preparation . . ."

A friend of Churchill said that Winston spent a good part of his life rehearsing impromptu speeches. One day Churchill's valet heard his master's voice booming out from the bathroom and stuck his head in to see if anything was needed. Churchill, immersed in the bathtub, cigar in mouth, said, "I was not speaking to you, Norman, I was addressing the House of Commons."

HOW TO PRACTICE A SPEECH THE RIGHT WAY

In speechmaking, one's situation is very much like that of a pilot flying an airplane. In flight, more things are happening at once than the mind can comprehend, and physical actions must be executed correctly with little or no thought. While the developing situation can be anticipated generally, subtle differences will emerge as the event unfolds, and these must be adapted to and handled. Consequently, everything possible must be "programmed into automatic," so that the pilot's mind is able to focus and act on whatever is different and critically important at the moment. This is a much more advanced mental process than simple memorization; it is a sophisticated blend of creative thinking and learned, patterned actions.

Preparation of this magnitude is accomplished through flight simulators that are an exact copy of an airplane cockpit. As the pilot operates the controls, the instruments react accordingly and resulting pictures appear out the "windows" of the aircraft, much as they do on today's TV video games. Anne Anastasi describes them this way:

"Their design emphasizes realism in equipment and operations. For example, flight simulators are usually built for each new major aircraft. These simulators reproduce with a high degree of fidelity the instrument panels in the cockpit, the "feel" of the controls, the sound of the engines, cockpit motion and other characteristics perceptible to the operator. To provide realistic practice in contact flying, a view of the runway and other ground features can be shown through the cockpit window by film, closed-circuit television, or computer generated graphics. Without leaving the ground, the trainee can thus perform all necessary operations for specified flight maneuvers. . . . Several investigations have shown that such ground training transfers well to aircraft flying and can effect considerable savings in costly aircraft training."*

John Hillkirk reported this in a story for *USA Today:*

"The veteran pilot flicks a switch to douse the flames with chemicals. It works. Fire extinguished. Engine back on. Problem solved.

"Nunn was never worried, though. The half-hour flight from Minneapolis to Rochester — and the fire — were simulated. Nunn was in Binghamton at the Link Flight Simulation Division of The Singer Co. to run final tests on Link's new 757 simulator.

"But all the while inside, it felt and looked exactly like a real plane. Close your eyes and you'd swear you're cruising at 30,000 feet or bouncing down an aging runway. The only dead giveaway is the cartoonlike display out of the cockpit. . . .

"When we emerged from the darkened, box-like chamber that sits almost ostrich-like on its six hydraulic legs, a half-dozen chuckling Link engineers lined up to show their approval — Olympic style. Each held up white sheets of cardboard, rating Nunn's performance from 1 to 10. . . .

"But there's a lot more to Link, a $500 million industry leader than fun and games.

"Link has built more than 150 different kinds of passenger jet simulators since 1929, when Edwin A. Link built the "pilot

*Anastasi, Anne, *Fields of Applied Psychology,* New York: McGraw Hill Book Co., 1979, p. 97. Reproduced with permission.

maker," a cockpit mounted on pneumatic bellows in the base-
ment of his father's organ factory."

As every flight maneuver is repeated over and over again in
both normal and emergency conditions, responses become automatic reactions rather than the product of conscious thought.
Experts who analyze the flight recorders after airplane disasters
report that pilots continue to function effectively until the
crash. As Dennis Grossi of the National Transportation Safety
Board puts it, "By and large, the crew is cool and just fights it
to the end. Any emotional comments come from others in the
cockpit."

When you practice a speech "right" you create the entire
range of conditions you will actually experience in giving your
talk. Practice is really total simulation, like getting your flight
experience before you take off. It makes a speech "old stuff"
even before you deliver it. ALL YOU ADD LATER IS LIVE
PEOPLE!

That's why you can come across as so relaxed and confident.
That's why you can concentrate more on the audience and less
on yourself. That's why you can put more of the best of yourself into it. And that's why practice is the good news, bad news
secret; it works beautifully, but it requires time and effort.

How do you practice a speech this way?
—By visualizing and imagining the entire situation in detail
  before you begin.
—By using a "pretend podium" and standing behind it.
—By speaking aloud and having the experience of your
  mouth, brain, legs and arms working together exactly as
  they will on stage.

Where To Practice

You need a place where you can be alone and talk aloud, at
least quietly, without being overheard. This is necessary so you
can give 100 percent of your attention to what you are saying,
and zero percent to worrying and wondering how others may be

reacting to what you are doing. A bedroom or the basement often works well. You will also need a "podium" so that your notes will be in the same position as when you actually give your speech. A cardboard box or a suitcase will suffice. Place the box on a freezer or a dresser so that you can stand behind it and look comfortably over your "audience."

Practice Takes Time

Whatever its cause, Americans have been afflicted with the notion that success comes to those who have great natural gifts or are very lucky. What we see on TV tends to prove it. "The great race car drivers and golfers walk, talk and look just like everybody else . . . except that they were born with the gift." This is a convenient outlook, because it permits us to relax in the effortless good life of waiting to see if mother nature or the fickle fingers of fate will drift anything our way.

There is no need to wait, for those who do have failed already. They have failed because they are watching the wrong part of the show! Success was achieved not by gifts or luck, but by the faithful, patient investment of personal effort. The golfer on TV was successful, not because of gifts or luck, but because of what he does seven days a week at 6:00 a.m. when no one is watching!

Olympic athletes are often average people who have trained with unusual diligence. Bob Richards, an Olympic medal winner in track and field, tells of investing 10,000 hours in developing his body and skills to world class standards. Think of that! How good could *you* be at something if you trained yourself for 10,000 hours? Thomas Edison said repeatedly that his success as an inventor was due more to perspiration than inspiration, that many people could have duplicated his accomplishments if they had but matched his effort. Michelangelo said that if people realized how hard he had to work to produce his paintings and sculpture, they wouldn't think them wonderful at all. And public speaking is no different! Most people probably supposed that Dr. Norman Vincent Peale delivered his great sermons almost "off the cuff." Hardly! Here's how he describes the sermon preparation routine that, for 50 years, required regular personal sacrifice and the faithful support of his understanding wife:

> "I found I had to think about it all week, devote hours in preparation and spend Saturdays saturating my mind with the message and nothing else — no social activity of any kind, no recreation . . . and this was painful. . . . But it was necessary if the sermon was to be any good."

There may indeed be a few people with great natural talents that propel them to superior performances with little effort. But the vast majority who excel do so because of honest, persistent work, and this must certainly be your approach. To envy the person with exceptional talent is to prepare yourself to fail.

What does this mean for you as a speaker? It certainly doesn't mean that you have to become a hermit and resign from the other parts of your life. But is most certainly does mean that you must begin thinking in terms of investing more time and effort in practice than you may have even considered before. The three minute speech for the White House luncheon took a full hour and forty-five minutes to get "just right." Certainly every talk will not, and cannot, require this kind of time investment, but practice is most effective and satisfying when it is pulled along by the vision of the speaker you want to become, rather than gauged by the clock or time of day.

Adopt the mental posture a good accountant takes when approaching a problem . . . simply planning to work at the task until it is properly done. Rather than starting out with a time limit, the essential attitude is to do WHATEVER IT TAKES to produce the kind of final result you want. Practice must proceed from the realization that your verbal image and your success as a speaker will be judged by, and only by, your total final performance. People will not notice or care how many books you have read. They won't know how long you have practiced, and they won't analyze your outline and gestures. But they *will* evaluate the total, final result of your presentation.

When investing this kind of time, be careful of the tapes you allow to play in your mind. Here are the ones that you must hear:

—Time is passing whether I do this or nothing, so why not do something worthwhile.

—The minutes invested in practice will have a greater positive impact on my life now and in the future than almost anything else I could do. The hours I spend each week in meetings, personal chores, idleness and repetitive work often bring small benefits when compared to this. It's worth the time and effort.

—Work expands to meet the time available; is anything really going begging because of this? (The answer is almost always no.)

Learn A Page At A Time

Repetition drives ideas and sequences into the mind, and this works regardless of your age or education. After repeating something often, one begins to remember it. It's as simple as that. Someone who should know is Michael A. Aun who says, "When I won the World Championship of Public Speaking for Toastmasters International . . . in Vancouver, British Columbia, I was interviewed by the Associated Press afterward, and they asked the key to my victory. My response: I practiced the winning speech over 300 times."

Repetition is most effective when one part of a talk is learned at a time, followed by learning the next part and repeating everything from the beginning. "Learn a page at a time," is a good rule of thumb. It works like this: Learn page one. Learn page two. Go through pages one and two. Learn page three. Go through pages one, two and three. Learn page four. And so on.

Be Natural, Not Perfect

Your goal is NOT to memorize your talk and give a "perfect" speech with flawless grammar, immaculate diction, every gesture in place and no stumbles. If you try you will fail and never become an interesting speaker. Many of the people you will hear, however, attempt nothing else. Most often they come off like talking mechanical dummies, and then wonder why no one is impressed!

What *you* must do is practice up to the point where you are self-programmed to be relaxed and "easy" with your talk. You want to come across as natural and spontaneous, full of energy and confidence. People should see you as an open, direct human being. You will do this by having the opening and closing portions of your speeches, as well as the beginning and ending parts of your stories, perfectly choreographed. Leave most of the rest, especially the middle sections of the stories, to grow out of your spontaneous reactions of the moment. This will be a natural product of having practiced with an outline rather than with a complete written text.

But how will you remember what to say? What if you forget? You won't! By the time you're ready to speak, you will have memorized the *sequence* of your talk so well that you will be able to enter it at any point and continue on. You will operate with "trigger" phrases, which are the first few words of a paragraph or section that launch you into talking about your idea. Once you have started, the thoughts and words will just roll out of your mind and mouth in much the same way as when you sing a song you know well. You will have more trigger words on your notes than necessary, and if the worst should happen, your complete text will be right there on the podium as your ultimate security blanket.

It is not unusual for an experienced speaker to forget an entire idea in delivering a speech of 20 minutes or more, but this is really not a problem. Good speakers know that missing one idea because they did not watch their notes closely enough is a small price to pay for the much greater audience impact they have by speaking more directly and from the heart. They realize that only speakers know what they forget; listeners are moved by what they hear and remember. This point of view may seem obvious, but from now on notice how many generally perceptive people choose to read a speech in order to say it just like they wrote it. Unfortunately, that is exactly what they accomplish, and the results are terrible.

FOUR PHASES

It is sometimes helpful to think of enlightened practice as occurring in four rather distinct phases as you prepare your talk. These are rough learning, outlining, smoothing out and final polishing.

Rough Learning

As you begin you will be trying to learn only the basic sequence of the ideas in your talk, or an awareness of "where you are" and what comes next. The rough learning phase is complete when you can read through your speech, take your eyes off the written text frequently and not be confused or surprised by how things follow along.

Outlining

Once you have the speech in mind, you are ready to prepare the outline you will use at the podium while giving your talk. Write or print clearly and rather large. Use a red pen to underline for emphasis if you want. Write the page number of each page of your complete text in the left margin of your outline. Here's something like what you should write for that part of the drug abuse speech beginning on page 127.

Pg. 1 — *Thanks Bruce . . . better than I deserve.*

— *When asked to speak . . . felt honored and pleased . . . admire and care.*

— *Since topic is on druge abuse . . . let's see . . . common experience.*

— *First, how many of us grew up in environment free of drugs? True for me too. Wasn't confronted.*

> — *How many of us feel know relatively little? Also true of me. Had no reason. Used time other things.*
> — *One more. How many of us have vague notion . . . temptation facing kids serious . . . should be very concerned? Also true of me. Never knew what to do. Have two boys. Love them just like all of us.*

Notice that the "outline" is really the sequence of ideas in the speech, but *not* all the exact words you will use in delivering them. Now take a piece of paper and outline the next part of this speech, beginning on page 128. Then turn to pages 152 and 153 and compare your work with my outline of the same thing.

Smoothing Out

Using your outline, go through your talk another three to four times, but now use more of your ordinary conversational words than your formal written English. Your goal will be to get your talk into "everyday American," so that people will understand you and know they are hearing an honest-to-goodness human being, not the reader of a formal document. Here's where a tape recorder helps. Simply record your talk, then play it back to see if it sounds like your ordinary conversation with three or four people. If it doesn't, keep "working the words" until it does. By now you will have nearly memorized the sequence of the ideas in your talk, and what you say will be sounding more like true-to-life you.

Final Polishing

Now your attention shifts to impacting the audience. You begin to add energy and drama to what you say, to emphasize certain words and phrases for effect, to add a pause right before you say something especially important, to pace your speaking so that it flows quickly without being rushed or slow, to say things like you really *mean* them. This happens usually after you've been through a speech at least eight times; when you know it well enough that you can begin to think about the audience instead of mostly about yourself or what comes next.

The final polishing phase usually begins with a sense of impatience with yourself. You just KNOW you can put your message across with more power and energy. You feel tired, as it were, of poking along on old city streets; you're ready to take to the open road! So you close your eyes, imagine your audience in detail one more time, see yourself eager and full of confidence, and then you begin again. By this time the adrenaline is running and you're having *fun!* Don't be reluctant to insert new words and phrases as you do this; the changes are one means by which you increase the drama and power of your ideas. However, if you make important wording changes, be sure to adjust your outline and manuscript accordingly.

GESTURES AND POSTURE

Chapter one (pages 37-38) includes a section on nonverbal communication and the fact that what people in an audience "hear" is actually overpowered by what they see and sense. The truth of this has given rise, mostly in times past, to concentrating in speech classes on specific gestures, proper ways to stand and how to indicate enthusiasm. This was undoubtedly the worst advice that could have been given. Nonverbal behaviors are so subtle and largely beyond conscious control that they are almost impossible to fake, or even to "program" through simulation.

The most effective way to incorporate the proper nonverbal signals into a speech, is to FORGET ALL ABOUT THEM. Work instead at learning your talk well, and saying what you want strongly and clearly. Posture and gestures will simply take care of themselves. Put one hand in your pocket if it feels comfortable; stand as you please; and do whatever you must to get your point across. Do what comes naturally! As a check to determine if your nonverbal behaviors are indeed natural and effective, you may want to ask a friend to watch your final, polished version and suggest corrections if any are necessary. But don't make any adjustments that would take you away from being your natural, positive self. It almost never works.

IF TIME RUNS SHORT

Chapter five (pages 112 and 113) explains how to get a clear and strong commitment for the time you were given for your speech. Despite this, programs often run behind, and you may find yourself with no alternative but to cut your talk short at the last minute. It will help tremendously if you have planned for this in advance. The best approach is to eliminate the least important of your supporting points and the accompanying story or illustration. Select the part to be eliminated and draw a light pencil line around that portion, so your eyes could skip over it to what you would want to say next. Then talk through the abbreviated talk twice in order to develop a rough familiarity with this approach. After that, forget it and concentrate on giving the full speech; if you've followed the suggestions in chapter five, you'll probably have all the time you were promised. But you're ready just in case.

IT'S YOUR TIME TO BEGIN

It's time to go to your quiet spot and begin. Here are the eleven easy steps to success:

1. Don't worry about how much time you will be spending. Give *yourself* and your future as much as it takes. Throw time at your talk like TV millionaires throw money. Your challenge is to give yourself totally to the experience of finding out how truly exceptional you can be with practice. Worry about being efficient only when you practice your tenth, not your first, presentation.

2. Find something about podium height on which to place the text of your talk as you have written it out. Stand behind this "podium" and close your eyes for three or four breaths to quiet your mind. Then imagine in detail

the complete situation. See the walls, furniture, people and, most of all, yourself. Hold it there and think of the person introducing you . . . feel yourself being the center of attention and being relaxed and calm.

3. Open your eyes and talk through the first page of your speech. If you come to a story, say the first and last few sentences as written, and fill in the rest. Repeat the process up through page four. If the *ad lib* portion of your story was too long or short, adjust accordingly the next time through.

4. Sit down for a rest, and talk through page five; then return to page one and talk through the whole thing again. Don't worry about how smooth and natural it sounds; remember your purpose here is to become familiar with the basic sequence of your talk.

5. If you come to a spot that is hard to remember, give it three or four extra repetitions. After you have worked through the whole talk this way, repeat it at least twice from beginning to end without stopping.

6. Now prepare the outline you will use at the podium. Follow the instructions on pages 145 and 146.

7. Return to your practice podium. Close your eyes and take three or four breaths to quiet your mind. Then walk through the visualization process again. Always do this when starting at the beginning of your speech. Then talk through your presentation, using just the outline and taking one page at each "bite." After each bite, start at the beginning again. Some of the words from your written text will jump into your mind as you do this, but many, many new word combinations will be created as needed. This is good, because the purpose here is not only to learn the sequence perfectly, but also to put the speech into your own conversational English. The trick is to know the exact sequence of ideas you want to talk about, and to avoid expanding on this when you speak.

This is the point at which many speakers tend to ramble, adding paragraphs rather than changing words. So, be aware of the danger and what you are doing; keep track of your time so that a 20 minute talk doesn't grow to half an hour or more.

You may want to change some of the words in your outline to be more "like you," and by all means do so. Using a tape recorder here will help determine if you are sounding like the person you have imagined yourself to be. Clean up the rough spots as necessary.

8. After working through the entire speech this way, repeat it completely twice from beginning to end. Be sure to repeat your visualization process each time so that everything is firmly in your mind. Continue to watch the time so length doesn't increase and become a problem.

9. Finally, pick out that part of the speech you will eliminate in an emergency, and draw a line in the margin around that part. Then run through the shortened speech twice, and get a rough familiarity with how it flows without the missing portion. Work at keeping the quality and intensity of the remaining parts identical to how you deliver them in the complete speech. Then forget it and concentrate on giving the full talk as you've prepared it.

10. By now you're probably feeling somewhat impatient with the practice routine and ready to conclude it. That's the sign you're ready for final polish! Do this the day or night before your talk, but not sooner. Start by taking one complete run through the speech (preceded by the imagination routine, of course) to refresh your mind. Then go through it at least twice more, adjusting the pace and adding the pauses and punch to achieve the impact you want. Let yourself go! You know what you want to say, and the words are clearly in your mind.

Now put your personal energy and strength behind it! Look right at that "audience" over your pretend podium, and say your words with poise and power. Be sincere! Allow your natural enthusiasm for your subject to take over. If you have a spot or two that seems to need work, give it as many extra repetitions as necessary. Tape record your complete talk now, and make final changes. Trust your feelings and gut reactions here. They are the best sensors you have.

11. After doing this it may be five to 12 hours before you give your talk. Always find at least 10 minutes within the hour of your talk to close your eyes, quiet your mind and imagine the situation and yourself in it. Then, look at your outline and mentally run through your talk just to refresh your thoughts.

Do It With Class

Now you're all set. Walk into the room with your notes under your arm. Smile, be casual and chitchat at will. You've been through this at least 20 times before, so stay cool. Greet the program chairman, take care of any final details and come across as relaxed and confident. You *will* be more relaxed and confident than you ever thought possible! Just try it and see.

SOME IMPORTANT QUESTIONS

This chapter suggests some nagging questions you may want to ask about now. Here are answers to some of the more common of them:

Question One: Is it always going to take this many hours of practice?

No. After you have given several speeches you will begin to develop your own techniques and shortcuts to save time. At the beginning, however, the challenge is not to be efficient, but to do WHATEVER IT TAKES to have the experience of being outstanding. Shortening practice time comes later and with experience, but even then the principle is the same: WHATEVER IT TAKES!

Question Two: Can I outline in my own style, rather than in the way suggested here?

The first time or two your notes should be very similar to the illustration. After that, feel free to change them a little each time as your style develops. But don't change too much too fast; learn as you go, and don't abbreviate too much. An outline should be able to give you all the support and protection you'll ever need.

Question Three: Can I take the chance of leaving my notes on the shelf under the podium before the program begins, so I can walk up with nothing in my hands?

There's no good answer here. If you leave them, they could inadvertently be misplaced. A good practice is to place your notes on the podium not more than five minutes before the program starts; then mention that you're doing this to the chairperson who will also be using the podium. (More than one chairperson has taken a speaker's notes after giving the introduction.)

Question Four: When I've invested all this time and effort in preparation, can I expect to feel totally confident and relaxed in the hours and minutes before I speak?

At the final polish stage it's normal to be wishing for another hour to make it even better. Adrenaline will be running and anticipation building. This is similar to the feelings we experience before any important event, and you should hope for the same. This extra motivation and energy are essential to do a good job, and they will vanish when you get to the podium. Then your subconscious mind, programmed by the simulation process, will take over.

Answer To Outline Exercise on Page 146

> *Pg. 2*   — *Pleased to learn from questions and answers that I'm a lot like you.*
>
>   — *Feel at home . . . talking to friends.*
>
>   — *As you may know . . . looking into problems of . . . year and a half.*

— *Learned much about serious problem.*

— *To show you what I've learned, come with me to L.I. Like you to meet Joan, Doug and Peter Benning. Tell story.*

— *After they found Peter's body, Joan and Doug went to the hospital to identify it. Met their pastor and a detective.*

— *Putting his arms around them both . . . led in prayer for faith, peace and strength.*

— *Then said, "In Peter's pockets they found two things. One was a syringe. Another was this note. In Peter's own handwriting it said, "Mom and Dad, I love you. Peter."*

SUMMARY OF ACTIONS TO TAKE

1. When you "practice," create the entire range of conditions you will experience in your talk. Practice in a place where you can be alone and talk aloud.

2. Throw time into practice like TV millionaires throw money. Do whatever it takes to get it "right." Worry about efficiency later.

3. Learn a page at a time.

4. Be natural, not perfect; never "read" a speech. Let gestures and facial expressions come from being yourself; never try to fake them.

REFERENCES

Page

132 You can map out: "The Champ, Joe Frazier," *Reader's Digest,* January 1972, p. 109.

135 Psychologists Tversky and Kahneman: Tversky, Amos, and Kahneman, Daniel, "Judgment Under Uncertainty: Heuristics and Biases," *Science,* Sept. 27, 1974, p. 1124.

136 Simon says that people: Simon, Herbert A., *Models of Thought,*
     New Haven: Yale University Press, 1979, p. 3.

136 Secord relates this to: Secord, P.F., "Stereotyping and Favor-
     ableness in the Perception of Negro Faces, *Journal of Abnormal
     and Social Psychology,* 1959, p. 313.

136 Also, remember what Festinger: Festinger, Leon, "A Theory
     of Social Comparison Processing," *Human Relations,* 1954,
     pp. 117-140.

138 Jack Valenti says this: Valenti, Jack, *Speak Up With Confidence,*
     New York: William Morrow and Co., 1982, p. 61.

138 A friend of Churchill: Gardner, John W., Unpublished speech to
     Independent Sector Annual Membership Meeting, Boston, MA:
     October 11, 1984.

139 "Their design emphasizes realism: Anastasi, Anne, *Fields of
     Applied Psychology,* New York: McGraw Hill Book Co., 1979, p.
     97.

139 "The veteran pilot flicks: "Link Never Gets Off The Ground,"
     USA Today, July 3, 1985, p. 6B. Copyright, 1985 *USA Today.*
     Reprinted with permission.

140 As Dennis Grossi of: Levine, Jeff, "Pair Find Answers To Air
     Crashes In 'Black Boxes,'" *USA Today,* January 24, 1985,
     p. 2A.

142 "I found I had: Peale, Norman Vincent, "You Can Choose To Be
     Bigger And Better," *Guideposts,* June 1985, p. 105.

143 Someone who should know: Aun, Michael A., "Cat Got Your
     Tongue?," *The Fraternal Monitor,* Chicago: National Fraternal
     Congress of America, July 1984, p. 31.

147 what people in an audience "hear": Exline, R. C., and Winters,
     L. C., "Affective Relations and Mutual Glances in Dyads," In
     Tonkins, S. S. and Izard, C. C., *Affect, Cognition and Personality,*
     New York: Springer, 1965.

CHAPTER 8
The Secret Of Object Messages

There are all kinds of everyday things
you can use to increase the appeal
and impact of a speech, when you
finish this chapter you will know
why they are effective and how
to find them. You'll also have
10 from my collection to get
you started.

"Hubert Humphrey's detractors accuse him of talking too much. That is unfair. His fault is that when he says things, he says them in a way that people remember. It's dangerous for a national candidate to say things people remember."

—Eugene McCarthy
Former Senator from Minnesota

THE SECRET OF OBJECT MESSAGES

This is the fun secret, a technique to be employed creatively and often to make your talks dynamic and memorable. With a little imagination you will be able to produce situations similar to one seven years ago that was part of an orientation program for district representatives, who were just beginning their careers with Aid Association for Lutherans.

These talented and aggressive salespeople were paid commissions for the insurance they sold, but they were also responsible for supporting AAL's local branches or volunteer groups. Most of the classes in the week long program were directly related to helping them succeed in selling. The one in question, however, addressed what many of them felt was merely "nice to do if you had time." Consequently, a primary goal of the class was to help them *want* to find the time.

Our team of four had three hours in a full week crammed from morning to night with one sales-related lecture after another. The seminar started on Monday, ended on Friday and we were usually scheduled for Thursday morning. By that time the class members had heard more than any mind could absorb; they were also tired of sitting and were eager to head for home. Often they were exhausted from a late party the night before, which gave rise to frequent comments about how our session would be a good time to relax and take it easy. Believe it or not, immediately before we started someone in charge of transportation would usually stop in to make a "special announcement" about their return flights home, which *really* put them in the proper frame of mind.

Our goal was to cut through all these obstacles and make a

powerful and stunning impact on people who could, if they wanted, give a tremendous boost to the branches. The entire three hour session was actually an expansion of the pattern outlined for 20 minute talks in the chapter on basic speech design; strong beginning, lectures (or content) alternated with lighter but powerful discussions in which class members could share experiences (or stories), and a powerful conclusion.

Did it work? You bet! Previously, the "volunteer" classes were so ineffective they were about to be eliminated from the program. Our team's first effort received immediate rave reviews; soon all classes were rating our session among the best of the week. It held this enviable position as long as the seminar existed. The session used every technique in this book in one way or another, but it was the object lessons that captured and made the strongest, most memorable impact.

Here's What Happened

Each person in the class had a desk with a name card on it. Usually they were piled with papers, notebooks and sales manuals collected from previous lectures. Before anyone arrived we'd place a salt shaker somewhere on every desk. Each of the small glass containers was filled with salt and "plugged" with aluminum foil so it wouldn't dirty clothes in a suitcase. Along with the salt shaker would be the agenda for the morning, plus a few materials we wanted to distribute in advance.

We would welcome people at the door as they arrived, and talk about everything *except* the salt shaker and our subject for the day. Folks would enter the room in twos and threes, wander sleepily to their desks and discover their salt shakers. Then, pondering it with a wondering smile, many would mumble, "What the heck is this?" Others would ask us about it directly, and we'd say something like, "We'll tell you later." Mostly, we would just go about our business, letting the energy build much like it does at a surprise party before the guest arrives.

In opening the class session, we mentioned that we would explain the salt shaker later. Then the attention it had attracted was *shifted* to the first topic of the day. By that time class members knew they were in for something special with people who had planned for their coming. They were awake and ready to listen — just what we wanted!

T Minus Twenty — And Counting

After a full morning of presentations and discussions the salt shaker on each desk was as mysterious as ever; by this time almost an irritating mystery. With about 20 minutes remaining, it was time for the conclusion that went something like this:

"At this time I'd like you to find the salt shaker we put on your desk. Please put aside all other papers and notes, and give me your full attention. (15 second pause)

"Salt is essential to life; without it we would die. But salt also changes things. Food can be flat, tasteless and boring, but with a little salt it becomes good. Salt sort of hides in the pot, changes everything and brings food to life. Now, the salt doesn't become the food, in fact we usually forget it's there. It more or less hides in the pot, changes everything and pushes out the flavor.

"And that's why salt is all about you. Our organization depends on volunteers to do things for others, because they want to. You help these volunteers want to do that

—by providing encouragement
—by providing help and support
—by helping them feel appreciated and self confident.

"In your territory you're like a pinch of salt, someone who hides in the pot and pushes out the flavor of our organization. You help people discover its potential . . . help them want to be part of it. If you try to attract excessive attention to yourself by being the whole show, the taste will be bitter and people will push it away. Nobody likes to eat pure salt. But if you can be just a pinch, *the taste will be good, people will sense their potential and you will succeed.*

"I want to tell you a story about someone named Tom Harding. Tom was an old man who lived in an extended care home. It was a nice place; food was good; it was clean; people were

nice; and things happened on schedule. Tom Harding lived in a room with six other men. As you might expect, they got along well, but also found things about which to complain through the long days. The major problem was that in Tom's room the contractor had built all the windows too high off the floor, and the men couldn't see out. Except for one window. This one was the proper height, but all the others were too high for the old and bedridden men even to get a peek outside. As you might expect the tradition in the room was that the person who had been there the longest got the window. And, as you might also expect, that person was Tom Harding.

"Well, Tom was a nice guy, and he tried to share with the others what he saw out his window . . . 'to brighten their days' as he told the nurse.

" 'Hey, here comes that lady with the grocery cart on her way to the store. Must be cold out today. She's wearing a heavy coat. Gloves. Yep, there she goes.'

"A little later he might say, 'Here comes that kid I was telling you about on Christmas Eve — the one who was kissing his girl on the corner under the mistletoe. He's running for the bus. . . . The driver's waiting! Has the door open for him. Yep, he made it! Sure was nice of that bus driver.'

"Then he might say, 'Hey, here comes my little girl. All prettied up in a blue coat, white hat and mittens. On her way to school. I wonder if she'll wave at me?' Then he'd wave his hand in the window, and wave again. A smile would spread across his face and he'd say, 'She's waving! She's waving! That's my girl! Cute as a button she is!'

"Early one morning a few weeks later the aides were in the room moving the beds around. Another of the men, Emmanuel, woke up and said, 'What's going on here? Why are you moving my bed?'

"The nurse replied, 'Tom Harding died last night, and you get the window.'

"Well, he didn't know what to think. He was sorry that Tom had died, but he was looking forward to having the window.

The aides moved his bed over, and Emmanuel slowly turned his head and took his first look. He looked . . . and looked . . . and looked. But he didn't say anything. The reason for his silence was that out that window was no street, no sidewalk, no buses and no people walking; only a long, low roof with a puddle, a tin can and an old piece of rope.

"Emmanuel lay back on his bed, and he thought . . . and he thought . . . and he thought. Was this guy Tom Harding the biggest liar there ever was . . . or was he the salt of the earth?

"Finally, he raised up on one elbow, looked out the window and said, 'Hey guys, here comes Tom's girl! . . . Wearing that nice blue coat and white mittens and scarf just like Tom said. I wonder if she'll wave at me?'

"He waved. And waved again. Then he said, 'Yep, she's waving! Tom's girl is waving at me too! Cute as a button she is!'

"You and I are very much like Emmanuel, because we make a decision each day, just like he did. It's the decision of whether we're going to stumble, mumble, moan and complain through each day, or if we're going to take our lives — you take yours and I take mine — and do with them what we can do with this salt shaker. And what is that? Shake it! Shake our lives to use our time, our knowledge, our energy and our caring, so that through us good things happen for other people. Shake our lives so that we become a pinch of salt for ourselves and others.

"One of the reasons you work for this organization is because you are a Christian. Jesus Christ said something about Tom Harding, Emmanuel, me and you. He looked at each of us and said, 'You are the salt of the earth.' He didn't say we might be, or we could be, or we should be. He said we are! When you get home, I hope this salt shaker will find a place on your desk, to remind you of who you are and of what life is really all about. I hope it will remind you about the importance of being a pinch of salt for others, including those people in your volunteer groups. And I hope it will help you remember that it's much harder for each of us to do this alone than it is for all of us to do it together.

Thank you."

Six Years Later

That story was told six times a year for about four years, often producing a sustained standing ovation at its conclusion. The last time was about six years ago. Yet, during almost every time I visit salespeople at meetings or conventions, someone says something like, "That salt shaker talk you gave meant a lot to me. I still have mine on my desk. Thanks for sharing that with us."

WHY DO OBJECT MESSAGES WORK SO WELL?

There are several reasons, one being that objects or things give people "hooks" on which to hang concepts or ideas. Tversky and Kahneman say that "salience," or the quality of being conspicuous or outstanding, affects the "retrievability of instances." They note that, not only are we more likely to remember such things, our judgments and conclusions are influenced by this higher level of recall. The experience with the "View From The Window" story is consistent with this. While undoubtedly one of the very best of stories, what makes it different than 100 others that people hear and forget after a time is the salt shaker.

A second cause for object message effectiveness is the well-known principle that review helps bring to mind what has been seen or heard. When a new idea or thought is worked through the mind within a day or so after it has first been learned, people remember it much better than something which they consider only once. Thus, the "madness of the method" included the idea that when the salesperson unpacked his or her suitcase at home, seeing the salt shaker would be a reminder of the story and the need to be a pinch of salt for the volunteer groups. Even better, the salt shaker might stimulate a family member's question, "Where'd you get this?," which would *require* that the story be remembered and retold.

Object lessons are also effective for still another reason. When used properly, they can add the fragrance of *mystery, anticipation* and *curiosity* to what is being said. Most speakers do not even think of these "powerful three," but you can use them to deliver messages that will stand above all others. The effect can be achieved in a serious business speech, just as it can in a club or luncheon talk.

Why? Primarily because the audience generates the effect out of its own human nature. You simply use whatever manner and style fit the situation, and let the object quietly work its magic on those who hear, watch and wonder. At a fun-filled celebration banquet, for example, you might put something near every person's plate and arrange to have the master of ceremonies make a humorous reference or two about it prior to your speech. (Be careful that this isn't overdone, however, or the serious message you want to send concerning it will be lost in the fun and laughter.) In a formal business presentation you could "hide" your object conspicuously under a tasteful cloth or box that is suitable to the dignity of the situation. Both approaches will produce the expectancy and inquisitiveness you want.

Finally, the power of object messages results in part from the power to hold people's attention on the subject at hand. Rather than wandering off into side trips, listeners seem to pay closer attention to what is being said. This may be because they don't want to miss the explanation, because an object simply makes the subject inherently more interesting or because speakers do something different and better when they are using one.

TO HELP YOU GET STARTED

Here are 10 object messages that have been successful over the years. They will help you off to a good start:

OBJECT	YOUR MESSAGE
1. Clear plastic glass	This glass takes on the color outside of whatever is on the inside. It won't do much good to talk a good line if we don't honestly believe it.
2. Six inches of heavy chain	Success results from each of us doing his or her part. Our success will be limited by the weakest part of our individual or organization's effort.

3. Shoes — Let's not be too critical of people in other plants, divisions or clubs until we've honestly tried to walk in their shoes for awhile.

4. Pencil and paper — Perfect illustrations for reminding two interdependent groups that each can be successful only in combination with the other. A nut and bolt also work for this.

5. Bell — Action, not dreams or good intentions, produces results. "A bell is no bell till you ring it, etc."

6. Piece of corn — This little thing is worth nothing, but you couldn't make one for five million dollars. God's power and potential are in this seed, and in you and your life too.

7. Candles — Light one candle from another to show how the best gifts of life are never diminished by sharing them with others. Use to illustrate the power of sharing love, motivation, encouragement, faith, etc.

8. Compass — Know where you're going! Replace aimless busywork with directed activity. Develop goals and a plan.

9. Electric light — Use to illustrate any relationship where one depends on energy from an outside source and must be "plugged in" to work. A politician must be responsive to constituents, just as a branch office must be to the main office, etc.

10. Clock or hourglass — Time is precious and not to be wasted.

HOW TO FIND OBJECTS FOR SPEECH ILLUSTRATIONS

People repeatedly ask me how continually to find interesting things to talk about. Here's the answer: Start by clearly identifying the major concept you're trying to get across; appreciation, planning, faith, teamwork, dedication or whatever. Cast aside the notion that object messages may be too corny for the dignified and rarefied atmosphere in which you will speak; remember the hoopla, informality and simple humanity that is part of the success pattern of many excellent companies. Then look around in your world for things that have these four qualities:

1. An inherent message: Something that by its very nature has qualities or properties that will illustrate your major ideas and help people remember them.

2. Commonplace: Something around the house, garage or office that people will recognize instantly and without explanation.

3. Inexpensive: Something so inexpensive that you could give one to everybody, i.e., piece of corn, paper clip, pencil, plastic glass, etc. (Not all the examples listed are inexpensive. Some, such as the clock and shoes, should be displayed and handled only by the speaker as a talk is presented.)

4. Simple: Something with an easy-to-understand function. An electric wire is better than a transistor, a garden hose better than a hydraulic one.

HOW TO USE OBJECT MESSAGES SUCCESSFULLY

Finding a splendid "thing" around which to build a major idea can fill you with the same eagerness and joy that you will experience when discovering a powerful story. However, an object message must be used correctly to be effective. Here is what you must do to succeed:

1. Position the object message near the conclusion of your talk. This will give curiosity and anticipation time to pro-

duce the desired effect. Revealing your secret earlier diminishes this impact, and can even make your conclusion anticlimactic.

2. Practice diligently so that you are self-programmed to handle the object smoothly and with ease. Work on this as hard and often as on any other part of your talk.

3. While practicing, carry out the exact picking up, putting down and handling actions you will use during your talk. Rehearse again and again what you will say about it while it is in your hands.

4. NEVER use more than one object message in a single presentation; if you do the appearance will be gimmicky, and the audience may become confused.

5. Avoid using an object message with every talk you give to a particular audience. Save this "ammunition" for the important ones; every third time seems about right.

Finally, be sure you present object messages with confidence and energy. You and your major idea must come out larger and more important than any object you use. How do you assure this?

—By drawing attention to it for only a few minutes of your total speaking time.

—By putting it aside before you give your last two or three sentences; design these sentences to focus on the major point of your speech, rather than on the object.

—By starting each practice repetition clearly imagining yourself as the confident and powerful speaker you will be.

SUMMARY OF WHAT TO KNOW AND DO

1. Remember that object messages increase recall and therefore influence subsequent judgments and actions.

2. Remember also that object messages add mystery,

anticipation and curiosity to a talk, thereby increasing audience attention.

3. Find objects to talk about in a speech, by looking in your own world for things that are simple, commonplace, inexpensive and that have an inherent message.

4. Position the object message near the conclusion of your talk; draw attention to it only briefly, and put it aside before your concluding sentences.

5. Practice diligently so that you are self-programmed to handle the object smoothly and with ease.

6. Never use more than one object message in a single presentation, and don't use the technique with every talk you give.

REFERENCES

Page

162 Tversky and Kahneman say: Tversky, Amos, and Kahneman, Daniel, "Judgment Under Uncertainty: Heuristics and Biases," *Science,* September 1974, p. 1127.

162 A second cause for: Bram, Leon L., Editor, *Funk and Wagnalls New Encyclopedia,* New York: Funk and Wagnalls, Inc., Volume 19, p. 440.

165 Cast aside the notion: Peters, Thomas J., and Waterman, Robert H., *In Search of Excellence,* New York: Harper and Row, 1982, pp. 263-268.

"Things may come to those who wait,
but only the things left by those
who hustle."

—Abraham Lincoln

CHAPTER 9
How To Handle Stage Fright, Hostile Audiences And Tough Questions

This chapter gives you practical approaches for controlling and eliminating three nasty problems. It shows you how to think about them before they occur and how to respond when they happen. After reading it, you will have a good foundation for handling fears that prevent most people from even attempting to speak before others.

"We can do most anything we want to if we stick to it long enough."

—Helen Keller

HOW TO HANDLE STAGE FRIGHT,
HOSTILE AUDIENCES
AND TOUGH QUESTIONS

Let's face it, while platform speaking increases your opportunities to serve and lead, it also increases the danger of public embarrassment. If you are not convinced that the chances for success greatly outweigh those for failure, you are unlikely ever to risk a major speech.

The destructive mistake made by almost everybody is that only weak, loser types worry about things like stage fright and tough questions. That is simply not true! Robert Nideffer is a sports psychologist who volunteered his time to work with Olympic athletes as they prepared for the 1984 summer games. At one point he met with the training camp's *top* performers and asked them, "How many of you have ever lacked confidence?" Surprisingly, every hand went up. Believe it or not, many of these world class superstars confessed that they thought, not occasionally but frequently, "What am I doing here with people who can beat me?"

Successful speakers fear stage fright, hostile audiences and tough questions, but they have found ways to keep these nasty gremlins in their places. Most of the people you know never get beyond condemning themselves for being fearful, and this becomes their greatest barrier to success. This barrier is more like a chain link fence than a mountain range; while the mountain range is impassable, the fence only keeps most people out . . . with know-how and persistence you can get over it.

THE ROOT OF THE PROBLEM

When you dig down past the specific fears and worries of any-one who is trying to accomplish anything involving other people, the root problem turns out to be anxiety. Almost all of us are drawn into anxious thought patterns so frequently that without informed effort we often adopt them as our normal way of looking at the world. "Informed effort" is based on the following facts:

1. Anxiety thrives on uncertainty, and one of the facts of any public performance is that you can never be 100 per-cent sure how it will turn out. More than 30 years ago psychologists were reporting that we feel less anxious after receiving bad news than when we are waiting and wondering whether the news will be bad or good.

2. We greatly exaggerate the likelihood of falling into horri-ble situations. The work by Tversky and Kahneman dem-onstrates that when we have vivid, imaginary pictures of some future event, we overestimate the chances that this will in fact occur. Public speaking is high on the list of what Americans fear; evidently our negative imagina-tions are working overtime.

3. Regardless of how good we are, we compare ourselves, not with our equals, but always with those who are slightly better. We seem never to be satisfied with our-selves.

4. Anxiety increases "task irrelevant" activities such as thinking about something other than the work at hand or repeating the same mistakes. We use this contrived "evi-dence" of our incompetence to justify our concern. This increases our anxiety in a vicious circle. Getting "cured" requires the same kind of conscious, faithful and enlight-ened effort one musters to lose weight or give up smoking.

STAGE FRIGHT

We were seated around a table at the community breakfast. Since several of us were on the program, the conversation drifted naturally to our public speaking experiences. Realizing that what she had to say was not breakfast conversation, one of the women at the table, who is a successful and capable professional, said quietly to her friend, "On the way to my first speech I stopped the car at a deserted spot on the road, got out and threw up. It was awful."

It does not help to deny that stage fright exists. In extreme cases it produces shaking, hives and all sorts of physical ailments that make public speaking literally impossible. More common symptoms are sweaty palms, headaches, tense vocal cords and shortness of breath. It often begins with mental pictures of being suddenly paralyzed and mentally blank before a critical audience. When this is envisioned over and over again, the natural pre-speech result will be a pounding heart, stiff jaw, red face or worse. Here's what you can do to eliminate or at least keep it well under control:

1. Use imagination exercises and condition your subconscious mind to give you positive thoughts. There are many books on the market about how to do this, but a readily available classic is *Psycho-Cybernetics* by Dr. Maxwell Maltz.

2. Self-program yourself for a successful speech following the detailed procedures in chapter seven (pages 148-151). A talented, professional woman used those techniques for the first time in preparing an important speech to community leaders proposing a new animal shelter. "It really works!," she said with pleasure and surprise at her relaxed and excellent presentation.

3. Learn to expect and accept *some* pre-speech tension as normal and necessary. Adrenaline flow will give you the energy to be fully awake and to do your best. Don't waste effort trying to feel before a talk like you do when watching TV; this is not supposed to happen, and it won't. Some professional speakers and actors experience even more extreme symptoms before "going on"; cramps, shortness of breath and upset stomach, for example. Once on stage, however, they relax and become models of poise and power. This can happen to you as well.

4. Use relaxation techniques. While these are very effective, they are anything but new:

> "But this is altogether the mark of the most common sort of men, for it is in thy power whenever thou shalt choose to retire into thyself. For nowhere, either with more quiet or freedom from trouble, does a man retire into his own soul, particularly when he has within him such thoughts that by looking into them he is immediately in perfect tranquility; and I affirm that tranquility is nothing else than the good ordering of the mind."
>
> —Marcus Aurelius

Harry Truman, who many said was less "aged" by the presidency than any other wartime president, said he kept his problems at bay by retiring to "the foxhole in my mind" where he allowed nothing to bother him.

Here's a pre-speech exercise you can use if your mind is a whirl of ideas and concerns. Find a spot to sit down, preferably alone. Concentrate on the air moving in and out of your body. Let your mind dwell on the rhythm, the feeling and the sound of your own breathing. Continue this for at least one minute. Then move your body into a position of perfect balance. Hold your arms in an equal and relaxed position close to your body, with your hands comfortably in your lap, not clenched. Sit erect with your feet flat on the floor. Most important, put your head in a position of balance on top of your spinal column; find this by moving it side-to-side and front-to-back until you locate that single position of perfect equilibrium.

Concentrate on your breathing for a few breaths, and then consciously relax your body by thinking about each part of it. Think: My feet are totally relaxed. . . . My legs are totally relaxed. . . . My hips are totally relaxed., etc. Then let your mind drift to whatever pictures are most restful and refreshing to you, possibly mountains, horses grazing, the sea or a beautiful landscape. Hold the picture in your mind and enjoy it. Do not think about anything else. The entire experience can take up to 30 minutes.

If done thoroughly, this "mental decompression chamber," as Maltz calls it, will produce much more of a relaxing reaction than you might expect. It will be best if you practice at least four or five times before your first talk, so that the procedure will be familiar and ready. Don't miss the fact that a shortened version of this can be done just about anywhere, certainly while you are sitting at a head table if necessary.

If you are determined to build a bright future for yourself, and if you use the techniques and procedures outlined here, you will overcome stage fright. It is as simple and sure as that.

THE SMART ALECK

Every organization has its challenges and inside jokes. One of AAL's was to reduce the flow of paper to branch officers. During the question/answer period of a weekend speech to branch officers in Baltimore, a well-dressed man in his early thirties raised his hand and asked an unrelated and stunning question: "I'm a branch officer, and with all the material I receive I'm wondering how much stock AAL has in the paper companies?" The tone of his voice and devious smile told everyone he was 75 percent serious.

Almost every eye in the room went into a frozen stare, and nobody moved. After an obviously long pause to grab a thought, I replied, "Your question is understandable; that's a problem we're trying to solve. We hope you can bear with us while we're working on it, and we *are* grateful for your help. Now, let's move on to other questions anyone may have on the new program we've been talking about. Are there any?"

Several people asked questions which led to an extended and helpful discussion. The man in his thirties said not a word. The workshop ended on a high note with the final two speakers from the audience finding clever ways to indicate that from their perspectives the paper flow situation was *not* a serious problem.

The man in his thirties was a smart aleck — someone who appeared out of an otherwise friendly, or at least neutral, audience to ask an antagonistic or loaded question. While a smart aleck may confront you in only one out of 100 speeches (that's been my experience), uncertainty arises because it's normal to think *this* may be the one! Consequently, it pays to be prepared with a general approach you will use. Here's one that works:

1. Avoid any negative responses. If you normally handle surprises and threats with anger or sarcasm, it will be essential to develop a different reaction. Imagine yourself responding in a helpful way. Self-program yourself for better answers to smart comments. Visualize yourself reacting this way several times before each talk so that you develop a "stay cool" button and learn how to use it. Don't be surprised if this begins also to improve your responses in everyday situations.

2. A "smart aleck question" is usually asked by someone wanting to attract attention and favor. The audience senses this immediately, and the person quickly isolates himself or herself from the group. After you have listened to the question or comment, respond calmly and confidently. Assume the person really wants to know the answer, and provide a mature, logical and friendly reply. NEVER react by attacking or ridiculing the questioner; this shows lack of respect for others, and the audience will also lower its respect for you.

    Present yourself as a helpful person, as looking out more for others than they may be looking out for themselves. Never be paternalistic or condescending. The result should be something with grace and a touch of class.

3. Close your response in such a way that there can be no further question from that person, and move on to someone else. The trick is to follow grace and class with a tiny

flash of resolve . . . to send a small but clear message that you will not be toyed with or trampled on. After responding with patience and care, the audience will understand, accept and support you in this. At the close of your reply say something like, "I hope I have answered your question. If not, please see me afterward, and we can talk some more. Now, does someone else have a question"?

THE HOSTILE AUDIENCE

You will almost always know when to expect a hostile audience. If you are a beginning speaker and have any choice in the matter, avoid these situations until you feel comfortable before friendly or neutral groups. Whenever you face a less-than-friendly audience, do the following:

1. Think through the learnings from the "foot-in-the-door" research. People are much more likely to respond favorably to a large concept or request if they have first agreed to a smaller, less threatening one. Recognize that, so long as you are completely honest and open, it is not manipulative to present your case in ways that make agreement relatively painless.

2. Identify the toughest and most damaging arguments your audience has with your position. Find this out by asking the person who invited you to speak, or by talking with a trusted friend who knows. Think through your responses to these questions carefully, and work both the arguments and your responses into your talk. This has two advantages, first that you will be prepared for the situation, and second that your audience will sense you respect them enough to have taken their concerns seriously.

3. Always begin *with* your audience by working extra hard to gain at least some acceptance and trust. Use the approach outlined in chapter two and begin by asking questions that bring you and the audience together. Your judgment will tell you what is appropriate. For example,

if you are a land developer speaking to a roomful of conservationists, don't open with questions about great vacations you've taken. You and your audience would likely have very different ideas about what makes a vacation "great."

4. Realize that people come to different conclusions for reasons which are sensible to them, not because they want to be foolish or stupid. Take the position of "walking beside" listeners to inform and encourage them toward better ways of seeing things.

5. Make the issue the problem, not the people. Take great pains to work into your talk statements like:
    —Good people see things in different ways, and that's OK.
    —It's good that responsible people care enough to disagree on something.
    —This is really an issue of (economics, theology, education or whatever); it's not a people problem.

6. Give your audience some of what they want, to open their minds for what they need. Make your controversial point immediately before your concluding story, and then use a story that illustrates your point and helps people see wisdom in it. Make your final sentence one which emphasizes that you want to work with your audience, not against them; end on a 'togetherness note."

Now, Let's Put These Principles To Work

Recall from chapter six the 20 minute speech on drug abuse for the service club? Well, this time you're going to give it to a local group that is angry about police brutality, and solidly opposed to supporting police departments for *any* reason. Your goal is to convince them to at least *consider* supporting better police enforcement of laws against drug pushers. Your original outline was:

Point C: Major thesis: Drug pushers must be stopped!
Point C: Story: Kids getting drugs at school.

Point D: First supporting idea: The nature and extent of the problem.

Point F: Story: Police chief from another town.

Point G: Second supporting idea: Police departments need our support!

Point I: Story: Phone calls to police chief and superintendent of school.

Point J: Third supporting idea: Family discussions about drugs are essential!

Point L: Story for conclusion: Boy devastated by pushers.

Thinking through the situation, you realize the outline will have to be modified. Since nearly every human being values children and family, you decide to keep the same major topic and first story. The original second story and second content portion (points F and G), however, must be changed to something noncontroversial; you don't want to talk about police departments until later in your talk.

You decide to move up part of your third "story" and your third content portion. At point F you will report on your call to the superintendent of schools and his ideas about what families can do to combat the drug problem. It will give you an opportunity to talk about a community institution that is not problematic for this group. The content section at point G will now be about families helping to prevent drug misuse. This should also be something about which everyone can agree.

For your *third* "story" at point I you decide to use the report about good police work in other towns; the final content portion at point J will include a call for supporting the police department law enforcement efforts. You will close with your most powerful story about the boy with a great future who was totally devastated in mental and physical health by terribly unscrupulous drug pushers.

The outline now looks like this:

Point C: Major thesis: Drug pushers must be stopped!

Point C: Story: Kids getting drugs at school.

Point D: First supporting idea: The nature and extent of the problem.

Point F: Story: Phone call to superintendent of schools.

Point G: Second supporting idea: Family discussions about drugs are essential!

Point I: Story: Phone call to police chief from another town.

Point J: Third supporting idea: Police departments need our support!

Point L: Story for conclusion: Boy devastated by pushers.

What You Will Actually Say

Since a flattering introduction is not likely, you plan to move into your questions without delay. Your opening goes like this:

Thanks, Don. I'm pleased to have this opportunity to talk with you about our community and our children. (Note the words "with" and "our" which bring people together.) *Since all of us care very much about both of these, I think it might be good to see what we have in common in this area. I'd like to ask you a few questions and then also answer them about myself.*

First of all, how many of us consider ourselves to be more concerned about our community than the average person? (Pause for a show of hands.) *OK, that's true of me as well. It's obvious that many of us here are involved in a variety of community organizations, and we feel good about that.*

You continue with two more unifying questions that emphasize the similarities between you and the audience, and then move into your first story and the body of your speech. As you expected, this first story about Doug and Joan Benning and their son Peter is the perfect way to drive home your major point that drug pushers must be stopped. After the first content section about the seriousness of the problem you report on your call to the superintendent of schools, and follow with the content section on educating children about the dangers of drugs.

No problem yet, but now for the tough part, the "story" and content they *need* to hear. You continue:

Another part of the battle against drug pushers is that we need to work with our police force in helping to eliminate this terrible problem. I realize you are very concerned about police brutality in our community, and I know this grows out of a deep and sincere concern for human beings and freedom. All of us respect that, and that is exactly why we need to work with our police against drug pushers. An example of how that can be done comes from Marysville, Ohio. (You tell the story and then say:) *It is important for us to try and make the same thing work here! Drug pushers are brutalizing our children, and destroying their freedom and futures. If our enforcement efforts against these ruthless parasites are paralyzed by conflict and anger, our children will pay for our mistake with their lives! None of us want that.*

I'm here to ask you to join me and others in finding ways for all of us to support our police department in enforcing our laws. I know you are active in our community out of your concern for human rights. Let's join together and develop a plan to protect the human rights of our children! They need us to do that, just like the children in Marysville did. (Continue with your concluding story and close with a one sentence statement of hope that you and your audience can work together in support of the children.) *Say "Thank you" and sit down.*

Notice in this speech that you are using the gentle art of persuasion; leading people inch-by-inch around to your way of thinking, and respecting them as you do it. Maybe you won't be able to convince them of your point of view, but you can earn their admiration as a person with integrity and respect for others. You may also plant the seed of ideas for change in the future, which is no small victory.

TOUGH QUESTIONS

If you presume to speak on a subject, certainly you should be able to answer most of the complex or detailed questions about it. Right? Well, yes and no. While you can be expected to be familiar with the broad principles and relevant history of your topic, there is no way to know everything. We survive in the world by using the information we have or can get to arrive at "good enough" answers to questions. Fear of not being able to answer tough questions can be overcome by learning two simple principles every beginning teacher, and every beginning speaker, must master.

1.   You know more about your subject than almost everyone else, and are able to answer most questions. Accepting only those speech topics you know something about, and carrying out limited research, will assure you of this. Depend on it as you begin or continue your speaking career.

2.   Descend from the lonely pinnacle of perfect knowledge and eliminate expectations that you will be able to answer every question. Give people in the audience credit if some of them are well-informed about your topic. Mention that you may call on them for help with questions to which you do not have answers. Expect that in any audience of 20 people, someone has read or heard something about your subject that will be new or unanswerable. If it comes up, be frank to admit you don't know, and say it with direct eye contact and no embarrassment whatsoever. If the question is one you think you could or should answer, consider an offer to locate it and report back. However, this takes time and effort, so do it only when you think it will be truly helpful to someone else.

This approach has worked for me for years in presentations all across the country. People have often asked detailed questions about programs or problems. In many cases I simply haven't known the answer; in others it was obvious that someone in the audience would have a better one. My response was usually something like this: "That's a good question, and I think we'll get the best answer if I ask all of you to share your ideas about this. How would you answer the question"? There hasn't been a time when this approach wasn't successful. "My" questions have been answered by scores of people who felt proud of themselves for having the information and being helpful. Yours can be answered this way too.

SUMMARY OF WHAT TO KNOW AND DO

1. Remember that we exaggerate the likelihood of falling into horrible situations. Getting "cured" of foolish anxiety requires the kind of conscious, faithful and enlightened effort one musters to lose weight or give up smoking.

2. Combat stage fright with imagination exercises, enlightened practice and relaxation techniques. Learn to accept some pre-speech tension as normal and necessary.

3. In responding to a smart aleck, avoid anger or sarcasm; provide a mature, logical and friendly reply. Close your response in a way that there can be no further question from the person, and move on to someone else.

4. A speech to a hostile audience should use the gentle art of persuasion and lead people inch-by-inch around to your way of thinking. Respect your audience as you do it.

5. Don't think you must be able to answer every question. Descend from the pinnacle of perfect knowledge. Call on your audience for help with questions you are unable to answer.

REFERENCES

Page

171 Robert Nideffer is a: Kiester, Edwin Jr., "The Playing Fields of the Mind," *Psychology Today*, July 1984, p. 22.

172 Anxiety thrives on uncertainty: Janis, I. L., *Air War and Emotional Stress,* New York: McGraw Hill, 1951.

172 The work by Tversky: Tversky, Amos, and Kahneman, Daniel, "Judgment Under Uncertainty: Heuristics and Biases," *Science,* Sept. 27, 1974, p. 1128.

172 Public speaking is high: Wallechininsky, Wallace and Wallace, *The Book of Lists,* New York: William Morrow and Co., 1977, p. 469.

172 Regardless of how good: Festinger, L. A., "A Theory of Social Comparison Processes," *Human Relations,* 1954, pp. 124-125.

172 Anxiety increases "task irrelevant": Marlett, N. J., and Watson, D., "Test Anxiety and Immediate or Delayed Feedback in a Test-Like Avoidance Task," *Journal of Personality,* 1968, pp. 200-203.

173 There are many books: Maltz, Maxwell A., *Psycho-Cybernetics,* N. Hollywood, California: Wilshire Book Co., 1977.

174 But this is altogether: Long, George, translator, *Meditations of Marcus Aurelius,* Mount Vernon, N. Y.: Peter Pauper Press.

174 Harry Truman who many: Maltz, Maxwell, *op. cit.* p. 177.

175 If done thoroughly, this: *Ibid.*

177 Think through the learnings: Freedman, Jonathan L., and Fraser, Scott C., "Compliance Without Pressure: The Foot-In-The-Door Technique," *Journal of Personality and Social Psychology,* 1966, Vol. 4, No. 2, pp. 195-202.

CHAPTER 10
Nine Questions
You're Sure To Ask

Before long you will probably wonder
about each of these nine questions.
They are the straightforward, practical
kind that will foul you up if you
haven't developed a thoughtful
response. This chapter gives
you that for each one.

"The secret of success in life is to be ready
for one's opportunities when they come."
                    —Benjamin Disraeli

NINE QUESTIONS YOU'RE SURE TO ASK

Chances are you have some questions left over, maybe even a few you think are fundamental to your success at speaking. The nine answered here will add to your speaking style and technique.

1. What about jokes?

Many aspiring speakers imagine great rewards from being able to tell jokes, a reaction probably created by the majority of orators who use them. The best advice is simple: DON'T TELL JOKES! In the first place, the technique has become overused and trite. In the second, while a joke may turn off carry over tapes, it simply does not develop audience acceptance and trust as well as the question and answer technique explained in chapter two. In the third place, although jokes in the body of a talk may provide a psychological break from the work of the "content," they generally do nothing more, because they do not power or illustrate your key ideas. Further, jokes do not provide the affirmation that helps to open the mind, thereby enabling people to listen to what you have to say; they can easily move audience thinking into the foolish, cynical side of life. Finally, jokes are dangerous; what is funny to one person may be insulting to another.

However, if you insist on telling jokes in your talks, it will be best if you follow these six guidelines for being effective and staying out of trouble:

a. Tell only jokes you have heard someone else tell with great success.

b. Consider the implications of each joke carefully; never use anything that could possibly create negative reactions in your audience.

c. Use jokes to replace your opening questions and/or one of the stories.

d. If you want to be taken seriously, never tell more than two jokes in a 20 minute talk; one is much better.

e. Practice telling a joke just as you practice a story. Rehearse until it's "just right."

f. The best and safest person on whom to tell a joke is yourself.

2. Any need to worry about how I'm introduced?

Yes, especially after you've given a speech or two and your reputation as a speaker begins to precede you. The worst introduction is one that creates such high audience expectations that even a superhuman performance produces only a "just what I expected" reaction.

To avoid this say something like, "When you introduce me, please keep it short. If you want to mention something nice, OK, but don't say anything about how good a speech I'm going to give. Let me earn my own reputation." For speeches that are very important to others and to you, write out the introduction word-for-word and ask the person to use it. People will almost always be relieved and grateful for your thoughtfulness.

Should you find yourself with an introduction that is too flattering and congratulatory, recover with something like, "If you knew how much it cost me to get him or her to say that, you would cry." Then ignore it and go on.

3. How do I find a topic when none is suggested?

This happens more than you might expect, primarily because someone wants to fill a program time slot with any interesting, helpful subject. In such situations, begin by turning off any tapes that may be playing the "I have nothing worthwhile to say" song and accept the invitation. Then make several lists that categorize your life. What do you do in spring, summer, fall and winter? What are the most interesting places you've visited and what did you discover there? What are the two most important things you've learned recently? Your answer to any of these could be the subject of an interesting speech.

Here are some additional ideas for specific topics or situations:

— Speeches for anniversaries and retirement parties: Focus on the people and the drama of their lives. Help listeners grow in appreciating themselves and the person honored. If someone was a fine janitor for 25 years, talk in a very sincere and honest way about how that is important, how it required perseverance and someone who cares, how the organization is better because of it, and how in carrying out these duties the person has performed as a responsible member of society.

— Speeches about your work: A speech can be created around any one of the following:

  • How my work has changed in the last five, 10 or 25 years
  • Things people should but don't know about my job or profession
  • How to get your money's worth when shopping
  • What my business needs from government in order to succeed
  • What people in my field are arguing about
  • Why I think my job is thé greatest.

— Talks for church groups: These talks, if on other than spiritual topics, should increase one's general knowledge and be fun. Be careful to avoid making inflammatory statements that could lead to unnecessary conflict. Some topics are:

  • Behind the scenes in my job
  • Church in my childhood
  • How the basics of my job can help a person or family (cost accountant, mechanic, oil executive, etc., could all provide helpful information here)

- • Teach and demonstrate personal skills such as exercise techniques, painting and managing time.
- — Presentations about hobbies: These can be developed into attractive general interest presentations. Talk about how you started in your hobby, its benefits and the secrets most people don't know about. Another approach would be to let the audience observe as you teach what you know to one or two children or adults.
- — Advocacy speeches: What are you concerned about? What needs to be changed? What persons, animals or plants need special protection? What groups need to cooperate more, *or less?* Where are you not getting your money's worth? What little-known facts or practices need public attention?

4.   What about off-the-cuff speeches?

You should expect, especially after your reputation as a speaker begins to grow, to be asked on occasion to "say a few words." When this happens, you need to do an effective job in order to be helpful to others, as well as to maintain and enhance the improved verbal image already produced by your prepared talks. Surprising as it may seem, many extemporaneous speeches aren't extemporaneous at all, and the better the speaker the less likely it is that *any* of the speeches are off-the-cuff! Some years ago Art Linkletter, Bob Hope and Jock Whitney, the American ambassador to Great Britain, were invited to the White House for a dinner honoring Prince Charles. None had been asked to speak, and as it turned out, none were called on during the evening. However, as they were preparing to leave Linkletter asked Hope if he had prepared something for the event, "just in case"? Bob Hope replied, "Are you kidding, Art? I'm always ready!" Linkletter and Whitney confided that they were also prepared.

Anytime you attend an affair where there is the slightest possibility of being called on for a few remarks, *have something prepared in advance.* Before you leave, take five minutes to jot down an idea or two. Think of a story you can tell to illustrate your point. Be especially clear and specific about the last sentence, which would be your conclusion.

If you frequently represent an organization at meetings, you may find it helpful to develop a "standard speech" of about five minutes. This short talk might bring greetings from your organization, mention a current major program or emphasis and close with a short story or illustration that shows why the company or group is important and worthwhile. Practice this just as you do any other short talk, prepare yourself to deliver it with power and style, and update it regularly as circumstances change. Then you will be able to relax in the knowledge that you are prepared at a moment's notice to make a contribution and to do it better than 90 percent of the people you know.

Is it worth the trouble? Absolutely, if you want to be a helpful, successful person! Your opportunities can be created in all kinds of situations and at any time; don't let a surprise cause you to miss even one.

5. How do I "read" an audience?

Good question! When an audience is "with you," the only sound in the air is your voice; chairs do not move, paper does not rustle and people do not fidgit or blow their noses. Your audience is looking at *you,* not around the room, at the floor or each other. Your eyes and ears "read" this kind of data, which leads to a sense, or gut feeling, about how people are reacting. As the attention curves reveal in chapter two, the audience will be most attentive during stories, and fade slightly during the content portions. You'll develop insight and skill about this, just as you have for other things you know how to do. All it takes is patience and a little experience and you'll be on your way.

6. Where should I stand in relation to the audience?

This may seem like a dumb question at first, but it's not. Sometimes when arriving for an event at which you are the major speaker you will find the podium too far back from the front row of tables or chairs. Its location, more than likely the same for every event, has in all probability been selected by someone who knows very little about giving a speech. You want to be close to your audience, not a voice from far away or on high. Always move the podium forward as much as possible. (This takes less pluck if you arrive early and can have it done before half the audience is watching.)

Try to position the podium so your face is well-lighted. Remember, most communication results from nonverbal signals, and much of that happens through facial expression. Your most important facial communication is the result of what you do with your mouth, eyebrows and forehead . . . with smiles, frowns, raised eyebrows or a smirk. Little or none of this will have an impact if you are speaking from the shadows.

Finally, a podium always comes *between* you and your audience. As early in your speaking career as possible, begin to move to the side or away from it, and talk directly to your audience without notes. The easiest way to begin is to do this with your stories. Request a neck or "lavaliere" microphone, or remove a stationary one from its holder. Then walk from behind the podium to tell the story. Begin this move at the beginning of the transition into the story, so that your physical change supports the shift from content into story. Then, move back to the podium with the transition from the story into the next content portion.

These six ideas will help you begin to speak without notes:

a.   Always know exactly when you're going to leave the podium, and program yourself for this through repeated practice. It should look relaxed, natural and easy-as-pie.

b.   Stories, like words to music, are easy to remember once learned. They "roll right along," and telling them without notes isn't a problem. You can test this for yourself by finding a way to tell your story to friends in casual conversation.

c.   When you tell a story straight from the heart and without notes, the impact on the audience is at least double what it is otherwise.

d.   The best story to tell away from the podium is your last one, where the greatest impact is needed. Stay out in front of the podium until you have concluded with, "Thank you."

e.   In a 20 minute talk, don't move from behind the podium more than twice, or your movement will appear patterned and forced.

f.   The worst fear you will have is that something may be unzipped or showing. Check yourself carefully in a mirror beforehand.

7.   Should I be concerned about mannerisms?

Yes. Awkward and distracting body or verbal behaviors draw power from your presentation, and must be eliminated. Have your spouse or close friend watch you either in your final polishing stage or during your speech. Then ask for honest, straight feedback. When asking someone to do this, be clear and specific about what you need to know and why it is important. Say something like, "I'd like you to watch me for unusual word patterns or any facial, body, hand or foot movements that appear out of place. It will help a lot if you spot these for me, so I can eliminate them." As you receive the feedback, be sure to exchange mutual glances and avoid defensive reactions; strive to be grateful and open.

8.   Where should I look when speaking?

Mutual glances help people feel they have had a successful "social encounter." Think about how you feel when someone talks to you but looks slightly away. Do you wonder if they feel inferior, doubt the value of their ideas or are uncomfortable around you? Do you develop the urge to grab them by the shoulders and say, "Please look at me when you're speaking to me!"?

Eye contact is more personal in a small group than a large one. With large groups you can look from side-to-side about halfway between the front and back rows. This develops the impression of strong mutual glances with listeners and avoids visually "bumping into" individuals. Looking at the foreheads of people in an audience also helps to create the right amount of eye contact.

With small groups, however, you need to look at individual people, and this may require conscious effort. Focus on shoulders and foreheads, which achieves the perception of eye contact while avoiding the psychological "bump" of a direct visual collision. This will be easier if during your practice sessions you visualize yourself in direct eye contact with men and women in the audience. Picture yourself acting forcefully and confidently as you peer directly into another person's eyes. The more you work at this the stronger your direct eye contact habits will become.

9. What about pauses?

A pause is to a speech what an exclamation point is to a composition. It draws attention and builds energy and anticipation, much the same as holding your breath. The pressure is released only when you resume speaking. To grasp the power of this, notice your own reactions when a speaker, or even the radio or TV, simply stops communicating for three to five seconds.

Insert pauses into your talks during the practice sessions in the final polishing stage. Position them sparingly, carefully and at key points for emphasis and attention. Timing is important, and you can regulate the length of a pause by your breathing. A slight pause is about half a breath long. A regular pause is approximately a full breath, and a long pause is two breaths. If you have the courage and want to have a major point scream off the walls, try a three or four breath pause.

Be prepared for the pressure build-up, and do not be overwhelmed by it. After you get the feel of this, go the next step and try a spontaneous pause to bring people to attention when you sense they are not listening closely enough. It works! Pauses are basic equipment for the verbal artist; learn to use them skillfully and with power.

SUMMARY OF ACTIONS TO TAKE

1. Instead of telling jokes at the beginning of a speech, use the question and answer technique described in chapter two.

2. Don't leave the way you are introduced to chance; explain what you want to the person who will do this.

3. Never play in your head the "I have nothing worthwhile to say" tape.

4. Have something prepared in advance any time you attend an affair where there is the slightest possibility of being called on for a few remarks.

5. "Read" an audience with your eyes, ears and gut sense; when people are attentive it will be completely quiet.

6. Position the podium as close to the audience as possible. Don't stand in the shadows with dim light on your face.

7. As early in your speaking career as possible, begin to move to the side or away from the podium.

8. Ask your spouse or a close friend for straight feedback on mannerisms.

9. Work on eye contact.

10. Pauses in speeches are the same as exclamation points in compositions; learn to use them skillfully and with power.

REFERENCES

Page

187 Further, jokes do not: Deci, Edward L., "The Effects of Contingent and Noncontingent Rewards and Controls on Intrinsic Motivation," *Organization Behavior and Human Performance,* 8, 1972, pp. 217-219.

190 Some years ago Art: Linkletter, Art, *Public Speaking for Private People,* New York: The Bobbs-Merrill Co., 1980, pp. 158-159.

193 Mutual glances help people: Friedman, N., *The Social Nature of Psychological Research: The Psychological Experiment as a Social Interaction,* New York: Basic Books, p. 56.

CHAPTER 11
Improving Your Performance In Meetings And Conversations

This chapter shows you how to apply what you have learned about platform speaking to other situations. It highlights eight specific actions you can take to improve your effectiveness in talking and working with others.

"I will pay more for the ability to deal with people than any other ability under the sun."

—John D. Rockefeller III

IMPROVING YOUR PERFORMANCE IN MEETINGS AND CONVERSATIONS

"School" makes practical sense because people can learn something in one situation and apply it to another. Likewise, what we learn with friends affects what we do with the family and how we work. This happens because psychologically healthy people function as integrated personalities with generally consistent sets of behavior patterns.

Psychologists call this "transfer of learning." It refers to what happens when your developing speaking skills change and improve what you do in meetings and one-on-one conversations. For example, you may make a point with a story or illustration rather than with only facts and figures. You may begin to choose words that send messages about feelings as well as ideas. You may relax more as you speak and use stronger gestures to emphasize your thoughts.

NINE ACTIONS TO IMPROVE YOUR EFFECTIVENESS IN MEETINGS AND CONVERSATIONS

Most learning transfer will occur naturally and without conscious effort as you improve your platform speaking skills. There are, however, nine actions you can take to become more effective in meetings and conversations. Try to make them your "old friends."

1. Do your homework. Know what major points you want to make, and have your ideas and illustrations well thought out. Organize your ideas and facts in advance; write this out in clear, logical statements. Remember that

people can keep in mind no more than five things at a time; if you have more than that, prepare a handout.

2. Use imagination exercises. Visualize yourself being confident and persuasive in meetings and discussions. Write one or two sentences on three by five cards, and read them to yourself each morning. While you read, create a mental picture of yourself doing what the sentences describe. Statements such as these will be helpful:

—In meetings I listen carefully and make reasonable and appropriate adjustments in my positions on issues.

—In meetings I exhibit a forceful personal and verbal image, and present my ideas persuasively.

—In one-on-one conversations I am an effective listener, a convincing speaker and a helpful, responsive person.

3. Practice saying your major points aloud, just as you do for a speech. Don't worry that your practiced words may not "fit" the actual discussion. It will be easy to make minor adjustments spontaneously as the meeting moves along. If this feels awkward or phony at first, recall Winston Churchill in the bathtub practicing his "impromptu" speeches to the House of Commons.

4. Replace complex, technical language with the simplest explanation and illustration that will get your point across. Remember that people reason two ways; rationally with facts and figures, and intuitively with stories and word pictures. Don't expect the necessary stories and clear explanations always to pop into your head in perfect form at the moment you need them. Create them in advance, and practice how you will say them in the meeting.

5. Use nonverbal signals that communicate self-confidence and respect. There is something delicately different here from what you do about nonverbal actions in a talk, which is to forget all about them. In a meeting, as in a speech, they cannot be faked or forced. But in a meeting you participate as a listener as well as a speaker, and you use nonverbal signals to send messages about what you are *hearing*. Exchange mutual glances with others, espe-

cially influential decision makers. Nod, smile and let your face show that you are attentive to what others are saying, particularly those with whom you disagree. Don't hide your face with your hands; better yet, keep your hands away from your head altogether. You will come off as stronger and more confident that way. If it is hard for you to remember this, write yourself a note and keep it in front of you during the meeting; use a code or symbol so others will not be able to read it.

6. Position yourself as a cooperative, helpful person; negative, blaming statements, which create defensiveness and reduce motivation, must be strictly off limits. Research results show that people who assume competitive roles quickly turn all other participants into competitors too. This changes meetings and conversations into psychological battles in which there are winners and losers. Your goal must be to find a way to help other people get what they want, and get what you want as well. Work hard at this and find ways to carry it off.

7. Listen attentively, not with "half an ear" as you take a side trip or contemplate what to say next. Work at it! When someone else has finished speaking, wait two or three seconds before making the next comment as a signal that you heard what was being said.

8. Take notes to aid your memory of the discussion. Write down a few of the exact words spoken by others; don't edit. In the margin write the names of the persons who spoke them. At key points in the discussion use your notes to summarize what has been said. This will help the group recall the original comments, will set the stage for you to offer new ideas and will increase your influence.

9. Make it easy for others to agree with you. Present and ask them to agree with smaller, less troublesome parts of your concept or point before presenting the more difficult ones. If you can be honest and sincere about it, express praise and affirmation of others. Find ways to agree with and help others get what they want and need too.

SUMMARY OF ACTIONS TO TAKE

1. Expect and enjoy the improved self-image that will develop as the result of being a better speaker than 90 percent of the people you know.

2. Know in advance what major points you want to make in a meeting; have your ideas and illustrations well thought out.

3. Visualize yourself as confident and persuasive in meetings and discussions.

4. Practice saying aloud the major points you want to make in a meeting.

5. Replace complex, technical language with the simplest explanation that will get your points across.

6. Participate in meetings as a listener by using nonverbal signals that send messages about what you are hearing.

7. Position yourself as a cooperative, helpful person.

8. Listen attentively, not with "half an ear" as you contemplate what to say next.

9. Take notes to aid your memory of what has been said, and use these to summarize the discussion at key points.

10. Make it easy for others to agree with you; compliment them when you can do so honestly, and express your most agreeable ideas first.

REFERENCES

Page

199 Remember that people can: Simon, Herbert A., *Models of Thought,* New Haven: Yale University Press, 1979, p. 52.

200 Remember that people reason: Tversky, Amos, and Kahneman, Daniel, "Judgment Under Uncertainty: Heuristics and Biases," *Science,* September 1974, p. 1128.

200 Exchange mutual glances with: Friedman, N., *The Social Nature of Psychological Research: The Psychological Experiment as a Social Interaction,* New York: Basic Books, 1967, p. 56.
201 Nod, smile and let: Chaikin, A. L., Sigler, E., and Derlega, V. J., "Nonverbal Mediators of Teacher Expectancy Effects," *Journal of Personality and Social Psychology,* 1974, 30.
201 Research results show that: Kelly, H. H., and Stahelski, A. J., "Social Interaction Basis of Cooperators' and Competitors' Beliefs About Others," *Journal of Personality and Social Psychology,* 1970, 16, p. 68.
201 Listen attentively, not with: Marlett, N. J., and Watson, D., "Test Anxiety and Immediate or Delayed Feedback in a Test-Like Avoidance Task," *Journal of Personality and Social Psychology,* 1968, 8, pp. 200-203.
201 Present and ask them: Freedman, Jonathan L., and Fraser, Scott C., "Compliance Without Pressure: The Foot-In-The-Door Technique," *Journal of Personality and Social Psychology,* 1966, 4, pp. 195-202.

"If you find a path with no obstacles, it probably doesn't lead anywhere."

—Unknown

CHAPTER 12
Taking Action To Change Your Life

To be successful we must know what
to do and how to do it. Then we must
do it! This final chapter shows how
to keep your attention, energy and
actions directed at becoming the
speaker you wanted to be when
you bought this book. It could
be the most important
chapter of all.

"People are always blaming their circumstances for what they are. I don't believe in circumstances. The people who get on in this world are the people who get up and look for the circumstances they want, and, if they can't find them, make them."

—George Bernard Shaw

TAKING ACTION TO CHANGE YOUR LIFE

The best things in life are *free!* In fact, the things that will change your life for the better are all free, and so simple they are almost corny. While almost everybody dismisses them as superficial, people of high personal accomplishment have almost uniformly taken the following two principles very seriously.

PRINCIPLE ONE: ACCEPT PERSONAL RESPONSIBILITY

YOU ARE RESPONSIBLE FOR LIVING THE LIFE IN WHICH YOU FIND YOURSELF. EVEN MORE IMPORTANT, YOU HAVE AN ENORMOUS CAPACITY TO INFLUENCE, AND EVEN TO CONTROL, WHAT WILL HAPPEN TO YOU IN THE FUTURE. That may be hard to accept, especially if you have not been active enough in taking charge of your own life. On the other hand, the fact that you are holding and reading this book may be an indication that you are close to accepting this, if you have not done so already.

The truth of this principle has been demonstrated thousands of times. Here's one example as told by Norman Vincent Peale:

"I had a letter recently from a congressman from the state of Missouri. He is in his fourth term, a distinguished member of the United States House of Representatives. His name was Ike Skelton. . . . At age 12, Ike had a very virulent attack of infantile paralysis which left his arms dangling helplessly by his sides. His legs recovered satisfactorily and he could function otherwise, except that he could not move his arms. . . .

"What he really wanted to do was be a runner. He entered Wentworth Military Academy in Missouri and went out for the track team. But the coach said to him, 'Son, you can't ever be a runner without your arms. They are almost as important in running as your legs.'

" 'Sir, I'm going to be a runner,' said Ike.

"The first year he went out for the track team and didn't make it. The second year he went out for the track team and didn't make it. The third year he didn't make it either. The fourth year the coach said, 'Okay, Ike, you're a member of the squad.'

"Then came the great event of the year. It was the annual meet of their arch rival, Kemper Academy. Ike went to the coach and said, 'Coach, I want to run in the two mile race, even though I know it's the most grueling of all.'

" 'Son,' the coach said, 'I'll give you any chance in the world that you wish because I think you're great. But you really can't compete in that race. However, if it is your heart's desire to run and that is what you want, I'll let you do it. I'm going to fasten your arms to your sides and then you do the best you can.'

"The race started. The first man came in. The second man came in. The third man came in. They all came in. But no Ike. The crowd waited. Finally, there was Ike, way behind, but he finished. And when he crossed the finish line all the students surged down out of the stands and rushed to his side. They didn't put the winner of the race on their shoulders. They put Ike on their shoulders and carried him around the track shouting his name."

Congressional elections are grueling races, and few people choose to run. Only a few of those who do are actually elected. But the boy with crippled arms did it, because he lived by "try" rather than "can't," and because he accepted full responsibility for his life and did something about it.

There are some simply excellent books that will help you know how to go about this. Considering myself "educated," I looked down my nose at them for most of my years and never cracked the cover of even one. However, since others I respected considered them very worthwhile, I finally gave one a quick and skeptical review. What a discovery! What a new way of looking at life and the world! If you haven't read any of these, or if you haven't taken them seriously, please do so soon. Here are two of the best to help you get started:

1. *Think and Grow Rich* by Napoleon Hill will help you claim whatever riches you want out of your life—fame, security, peace of mind or wealth. The story of this book is told in the publisher's preface:

   "It was inspired by Andrew Carnegie who disclosed his formula of personal achievement to the author, Napoleon Hill, many years ago. Carnegie not only made himself a multi-millionaire, but he made millionaires of more than a score of men to whom he taught his secret. Another 500 wealthy men revealed the source of their riches to Napoleon Hill, who spent a lifetime of research in bringing their message to people in all walks of life . . ."*

   Think and Grow Rich is now available in paperback from Fawcett Publications, Inc., of Greenwich, Connecticut. It was first published in 1937 and has stood the test of time.

2. *I Dare You* was written by William H. Danforth who was founder and head of the Ralston Purina Company in St. Louis. It was first published in a limited edition for the benefit of his business, family and personal friends. Here, from the foreword of the book is the rest of the story:

   "Each book passed many times from one person to another. The idea spread and affected people of all ages and in all walks of life. . . . The demand from sales managers, YMCA secretaries, business executives, college organizations, vocational teachers, personnel and guidance workers, preachers—everyone whose aim it is to challenge men and women to superior accomplishment—soon exhausted the early edi-

*From *Think And Grow Rich* by Napoleon Hill. Copyright © 1967, 1966, 1960, 1937 by The Napoleon Hill Foundation. A Hawthorn book. Reprinted by permission of E. P. Dutton, a division of New American Library.

tions. Now comes the twenty-seventh edition. Here is more than a book. It is a working pattern of life written out of a pioneer business man's own rich experience. . . . It is a practical plan for action for everybody who wanted to go somewhere, be somebody and be of service."**

PRINCIPLE TWO: GOALS CHANGE LIVES

WHAT WE RECEIVE FROM LIFE WILL BE AN EXACT REFLECTION OF OUR GOALS AND EXPECTATIONS FOR IT. STATED ANOTHER WAY: IF YOU WANT TO CHANGE THE REST OF YOUR LIFE, CHANGE YOUR GOALS AND EXPECTATIONS. Here are the important basic ideas:

1. Every person has goals or expectations for life. These are almost always unwritten, and they may be unknown. Nevertheless, they are life's controlling forces; we always become the persons we set out to be.

2. Psychologists studying the effect that goals have on success or failure have made important discoveries. First, Locke tested male and female subjects in a simple experiment involving math problems. He found that people achieve more when they have a specific goal to reach for than when they are told simply to, "Do your best." Second, in other research it was found that after people achieve one goal they feel more confident that other similar goals are attainable. Third, a study by Waterman and Ford revealed that people pay closer attention to a task when they believe a goal is attainable; when they believe it is impossible they lose interest and do not attend to the details of the work. The implications of this for anyone who wants to succeed are that we must establish goals,

**Reprinted by permission of the American Youth Foundation, 1415 Elbridge Payne Rd., St. Louis, MO 63017. Copies of *I Dare You* can be ordered from the "I Dare You" Committee, 835 S. Eighth St., St. Louis, MO 63188.

and that these goals must be attainable with reasonable effort.

3. A goal is not merely a notion or passing thought. It is NOT something one can have without giving up something else. You might, for example, say you want more money, but if you continue to watch TV three hours every night, then leisure is your goal, not more money. When a goal is accepted and strongly desired, it secures *commitment, preference* and *action* in your life. If it does not, it is simply not a goal.

4. Growth or "stretch" goals add purpose to life. They give a sense of balance with which one can move forward, just as when riding a bicycle. With stretch goals you squeeze more out of each day, you are happier and your priorities and focus are much clearer. Without them life loses its forward motion, energy, poise and tone. As Russell Jones puts it, "One of the strongest messages that comes across when people are questioned about their lives and their work is that a steady diet of pointless activity deadens the spirit. Life becomes tasteless, odorless and flat."

5. Goals must be specific and *written.* Identify the exact habit, thing or quality you want to acquire and by when. Then write it on a three by five card and post it where you will see it often.

6. Goals must present a challenge. Don't set goals you know you can achieve with minimal effort. Establish those that will pull you up and out to greater and greater achievements.

CAN YOU AFFORD NOT TO TRY?

Consider what experimental psychology has uncovered about the unseen forces of the particular world in which you are living right now. Here are the four major ideas:

1. WE ARE NOT THE ANALYTICAL, RATIONAL THINKERS WE BELIEVE OURSELVES TO BE, AND

WE JUMP TO CONCLUSIONS USING SKIMPY IN-
FORMATION AND SIMPLE RULES OF THOUGHT.

The important implications of this for your decisions about
public speaking are these: People draw conclusions about us
on the basis of what they can readily observe or find out, and on
the basis of what they know about people with similar qualities.
Regardless of how capable you are, it is impossible for most
people to make an informed judgment about that; they have no
choice but to fill in the blanks about your potential and ability
on the basis of what is superficially apparent. A good speech
puts your "best foot forward" and helps people reach favorable
conclusions about your ability and potential.

2.   AFTER MAKING A FAULTY JUDGMENT, WE LOOK
     FOR EVIDENCE THAT WILL CONFIRM OUR UN-
     FOUNDED CONCLUSION. WE STICK TO OUR
     MISTAKES.

This partly irrational process is the way human beings make
what Tversky and Kahneman term "illusory correlations"
about the people and events in their lives. After giving an exceptional speech it is not unusual to notice that some of your listeners are more open to other of your ideas and suggestions.
Their favorable impressions of your talk will have lead them to
more positive evaluations of you and your work. Next, they will
collect further "evidence" about you that supports their new,
more positive insights.

Consequently, we need to work hard at the impressions we
make on others, and we should not discount the determining
importance of our first impressions. Whatever people choose to
think and decide about us will be influenced by the "information" they collect first, and this "information" will be shaped
more by opinion than by fact.

On the other hand, if you've been making some negative impressions, you may be tempted to throw in the towel and quit.
At the very least you may conclude that the best hope of success
would be to develop your speaking skills, leave your present situation and start over with different people in a new place. There

may be some value in that, since as research by Dailey reveals, after people make a premature judgment with limited data they resist or ignore information that would cause them to change their minds.

But it isn't that bleak. Countless studies and our own experiences also suggest that people are continually adding new information to whatever they know. Change is a wonderful fact of life. If you begin to speak well, many things about the original notion or stereotype people have of you will no longer make sense, especially in light of consistently better performance. In the reevaluation process that follows, they will find many reasons to select and use different pieces of information that fit with their newer, albeit superficial, notions about you. With effort and a little luck you will have many opportunities to make a better impression; one good experience will build on and reinforce the next.

3. WE BEHAVE IN WAYS THAT FIT WITH WHAT WE BELIEVE OTHERS THINK OF US.

People are led to conclusions about us on the basis of our self perceptions. If we reach an incorrect conclusion that we are failing, we encourage others to treat us that way. When they do, this "proof" reinforces our false perceptions, and the whole circle of thoughts and events becomes a vicious trap. We have no choice but to prove, first to ourselves and then to others, that we are truly capable. The joy of being a helpful person, the applause, the expressions of appreciation and responding to requests for our advice about other problems; all this will help us stand better and taller in our own eyes. We then will improve our actions and behaviors in other areas of life. This is truly a powerful benefit of becoming a good speaker, and there is every reason to expect it will happen to you.

4. IRRATIONAL BEHAVIOR IS A FACT OF LIFE EVERYWHERE — CORPORATIONS, GOVERNMENT, ASSOCIATIONS, VOLUNTEER GROUPS, ETC.

Professionals who have been trained to know better also behave irrationally. Studies are filled with examples of lawyers, psychiatrists, teachers and clinical psychologists making all the mistakes that we usually ascribe only to the uninformed John or Jane Doe.

Daniel Isenberg of Harvard Business School analyzed the thinking processes used by senior managers, spending from one to 25 days studying each of 12 people in six corporations. Isenberg describes the managerial mind as "imperfectly rational," and urges us to curb our overly ambitious expectations for something better. His description of how managers think bears a striking resemblance to Simon's discovery of patterns or vocabularies of thought, and to the idea that people have no choice but to find "good enough" solutions to problems. Isenberg says managers use intuition to bypass in-depth analysis and move rapidly to plausible solutions. They work on issues until they find matches between "their guts and their heads."

What this means is that all of us are people before we are employees, volunteers, executives or anything else, and that the beauty and the foibles of the human mind are present in every situation. The bad news is that there is no escape; the good news is that the rules are the same everywhere, and for everyone.

HOW NOT TO FALL FLAT ON YOUR FACE

In reading this book you have discovered how public speaking can enhance your career, influence, self-respect, attractiveness and more. Every bit of it is true! Just as important is that the book also contains even more references to becoming a public speaker out of a strong desire to be *helpful* to others. If your most basic desire in giving a speech is to be useful to and supportive of others, then all the benefits of better career, influence, higher income and more can naturally result. However, these benefits will escape your grasp like fog in the air if seeking them becomes your primary goal. Audiences size up speakers quickly and rather accurately. If you are perceived as mostly serving your own interests or feeding your ego, the results will likely be very negative for you.

HOW TO ESTABLISH YOUR GOALS

First of all, take time to identify your present goals . . . the ones that now govern your life and are expressed in the way you spend your time and money. Think about them for two or three days and decide whether or not you want to make any changes. The honest answer may be no. However, if it is yes, begin by thinking about what you want to do with the rest of your life. Where will you live? What kind of work will you do? How will you serve others? How much will you earn? What amount will you contribute to church and charity? You need these big goals to give your life stretch and focus. As you do this it will help to remember the words of Daniel H. Burnham:

"Make no little plans. They have no magic with which to stir the blood and probably themselves will not be realized. Make big plans; aim high in hope and work. Remember that our children and grandchildren will do things that would stagger us. Remember that when you create a situation that captures the imagination, you capture life, reason, everything."

To reach these larger goals you also need smaller ones. What will you accomplish by one year from today? How much time will you devote to what is most important to you? By when will you give your first speech, or your next report at work? Don't shrink back from setting these goals because at the moment you see no way to achieve them. Simply setting the goal will begin to draw your energy and attention to finding the answer in due time. Let that answer come as events unfold and your subconscious mind goes to work on the problem. Keep this in mind:

"There is no such thing as a self-made man.
I've had much help and have found that if
you are willing to work, many people are
willing to help you."
—O. Wayne Rollins

Let's say that one of your goals is to give a six to eight minute speech within two months. This is a high quality goal for a number of reasons:

— It is SPECIFIC about what you will do; give a six to eight minute speech.

— It has a TIME LIMIT by when this will happen; within two months.

— It AVOIDS SPECIFICS ABOUT HOW you will do this; questions about speech topic, where it will be given and to how many people remain unanswered.

— It is REALISTIC; two months should give you adequate time to reach the goal.

— It is CHALLENGING; you will have to take action if the goal is to be achieved.

Remember that goals must be WRITTEN DOWN AND REVIEWED REGULARLY. This will prevent them from being rationalized away as something you "really didn't want to do anyway." Set the goal for giving your first or next talk immediately. Please lay this book aside right now, and write out your goal. Then post it where you will see it each morning, say on the bathroom mirror.

Opportunities Abound!

If you have now established a goal for giving a first or next speech, you will have a tremendous number of opportunities to achieve it. It is likely that you have interests or concerns, all of which could lead to a topic; taxes, education, unemployment, drugs, stamp collecting or chess, for example. Maybe you're a business type who could give a presentation to people who want to start their own companies. A reporter might speak to journalism classes at area high schools. A skilled homemaker might speak to home economics classes. Churches and service clubs are *always* looking for speakers. The list is endless. Don't be surprised if your opportunity comes from unexpected places, and don't be reluctant to share this goal with others, especially people like your pastor, a few friends, trusted work associates and maybe your boss. What you say starts people thinking about how you could help them or help others! Just try it and see what develops.

Araid? OK, so are lots of people. But those who succeed are the ones who do it anyway. In the words of Frederick B. Wilcox:

> "Progress always involves risk. You can't steal second base and keep your foot on first."

PEEL YOUR ONION

Learning is an intensely personal process. No one can do it for us, and we must always start from where we are. Learning is like peeling an onion, layer by layer. We move on to the next level of competence or knowledge only after we master the prior one. From time to time we slide back to rummage around again in the scraps of previous layers before going on to peel again. It's possible to stop learning anywhere along the way, and many do. Of course, the speed and success with which we learn will vary greatly, depending on our energy, time investment and information resources. Nevertheless, the process remains individual and sequential. Everyone has to do his or her own learning, and YOU will decide if this is fun or a chore. It must be the former if you are to succeed.

THE RULE OF TWENTY-FIVE

Whenever a goal leads you into doing something new, it feels uncomfortable and strange for some time. We are told by psychiatrists that it takes about 25 days to change a habit or behavior. Unfortunately, many people fail to realize this, and consequently evaluate a new habit or experience much too soon. Until reading *Psycho-Cybernetics* I did this consistently. Shortly thereafter I decided that my practice of jogging on the roadway pavement was not good, and that I should run on the gravel shoulder instead. Using what I had learned, I decided to run on the shoulder for 25 days before even *beginning* to evaluate whether I liked it or not. My promise to myself was: Do it for 25 days, then decide.

I remember the first few runs being absolutely terrible! The stones were not smooth like the pavement; the shoulders were

more sloped and not as firm; and the potholes turned into pud-
dles after a rain. If I had used my customary procedure of deciding after three or four days, I would certainly have returned to
running on the pavement. But after 25 days, I was accustomed
to the shoulder. The stones no longer felt rough; I had developed stronger ankles to handle the slope and loose footing; and
I had learned to run easily around the potholes. Shoulders are a
safer, better place to run, and I'm still using them, thanks to the
rule of 25.

It is important for you to do the same with any new habit or
behavior you want to develop. The 25 day minimum will move
you through the stages of novelty and awkwardness, and
position you to evaluate an alternative habit or action correctly.
If it's not acceptable, you will reject it for the proper reasons,
not merely because it is unfamiliar. The principle of avoiding
premature decisions can also help you avoid the trap of making
too many judgments about your speaking ability until you have
given at least four or five talks and have a better idea of how to
go about it.

Above all, be patient with yourself. There will be what
Olympic athletes call "setbacks." Your progress will look like a
jagged line in a generally upward direction, not a smooth,
sweeping arc to the top. Realize that the secret of success in any
endeavor is more persistence than talent or training. The
world's greatest artists, leaders and inventors are uniform in
their commitment to perseverance. Practice "successful
failure," which is the habit of using failure as a source of
learning and growth, rather than defeat. Two quotes about this
are particularly helpful.

> "The only time you fail is the last time you
> try."

> "Nothing in the world can take the place of
> persistence. Talent will not; nothing is more
> common than unsuccessful men with talent.
> Genius will not; the world is full of educated
> derelicts. Persistence and determination
> alone are omnipotent. The slogan 'press on'

has solved and always will solve the problems of the human race.''
—Calvin Coolidge

GO FOR IT!

My friend and I had been planning a sailing trip for months.
The day finally came, and it was cold, rainy and very windy. We
loaded the boat and decided to wait for an hour. Sixty minutes
later everything was the same, and I was almost ready to suggest
that maybe we should call the whole thing off. Then Armon
said, ''We've wanted to do this. You have the goal to sail to that
new harbor this summer. Let's go for it!''

We moved away from the mooring, set the sails in a driving
wind and rain, and headed out on that lonely lake for a strange
port 16 miles away. My feelings were mixed; glad to be on the
way, generally confident but also tense and concerned. Two
hours later we rounded the Long Point buoy and headed south.
In two more hours we were tied up in Fond du Lac harbor,
drinking wine and toasting our achievement. It's an experience
not to be forgotten — ever!

Your situation may be quite the same. After you've finished
the book, there comes a time when you must take the risk of giving your first or next speech. If you fail to do this, you will
probably resign yourself to the ranks of the professional students who prepare, practice, learn, study, rehearse but never
do. You will have the boat all packed and ready, but never leave
the harbor. You will be saying, ''One for the money, two for the
show, three to get ready, four to get ready, five to get ready and
on and on. The challenge of a first effort is not to do it effi-
ciently or even excellently; it is simply to begin and complete it
in the confident hope that from humble beginnings great things
can happen. What has happened to others may happen to you:

> ''In the spring of his first year at Boston, word came
> that the Methodist church in the little town of Walpole,
> Massachusetts, needed someone to fill its pulpit on
> Sunday. . . . For two full weeks he worked feverishly on

his sermon, writing and rewriting it. For a text he chose his father's favorite: 'I am come that they might have life, and that they might have it more abundantly.'

"He prepared his sermon in at least seven different versions. None of them seemed to him to have the slightest merit. Finally, on the Monday before the dreaded Sunday, he wrote in panic to his father. 'I wish,' he said, 'that you would send me your notes, or any written copy you may have of the sermon I have heard you preach so often on this text. I want so much to do a worthwhile job at Walpole. Please send me anything you have *at once!*'

"He did not have to wait long for a reply; it came by return mail in his father's familiar scrawl: 'Prepare your own sermons. Just tell the people that Jesus Christ can change their lives. Love, Dad.'

"With this gentle kick still tingling in the seat of his spiritual pants, Norman went down to Walpole."

"Norman," as you have probably guessed, grew from that to become none other than the famous minister and speaker, Dr. Norman Vincent Peale. You and I have but one life to live, and today is the first day of the rest of it. As my friend Armon said to me as we sat huddled in that rainy harbor, "LET'S GO FOR IT!"

I wish you well.

Godspeed,

John Dutton

SUMMARY OF WHAT TO KNOW AND DO

1. Accept personal responsibility; take charge of your life!

2. Goals change lives, and they must be specific and written. Identify the exact habit, thing or quality you want to acquire and by when.

3. We are not the analytical, rational thinkers we believe ourselves to be. We jump to conclusions using skimpy information and simple rules of thought.

4. After making a faulty judgment we look for evidence that confirms our unfounded conclusion. We stick to our mistakes.

5. We behave in ways that fit with what we believe others think of us.

6. Irrational behavior is a fact of life everywhere — corporations, government, associations, volunteer groups, etc.

7. Give speeches to be helpful, not simply for personal gain or ego gratification.

8. Speaking opportunities abound; don't be surprised if they come from unexpected places.

9. Progress always involves risk.

10. Learning is an intensely personal process. No one can do it for us, and we must always start from where we are.

11. It takes about 25 days to change a habit or behavior.

12. The only time you fail is the last time you try.

13. Go for it!

REFERENCES

Page

207 "I had a letter: Copyright © 1984 by the Foundation for Christian Living. Reprinted from *PLUS: The Magazine of Positive Thinking.* May 1984, pp. 8-10. Copies of this publication are available from PLUS, P. O. Box FCL, Pawling, New York 12546.

210 First, Locke tested male: Locke, E. A., "Motivational Effects of Knowledge of Results: Knowledge or Goal Setting?" *Journal of Applied Psychology,* 1967, 51, pp. 324-329.

210 Second, in other research: Child, I. L., and Whiting, J. W, "Effects of Goal Attainment: Relaxation Versus Renewed Striv-

ing," *Journal of Abnormal and Social Psychology,* 1950, 45, pp. 667-681.

210 Third, a study by: Waterman, A. S., and Ford, L. H., "Performance Expectancy as a Determinant of Actual Performance: Dissonance Reduction or Differential Recall," *Journal of Personality and Social Psychology,* 1965, 2, pp. 464-467.

211 As Russell Jones puts: Jones, Russell A., *Self-Fulfilling Prophecies,* Hillsdale, New Jersey: Lawrence Erlbaum Associates, 1977, p. 198.

211 We are not the:
   1. Simon, Herbert A., *Models of Thought,* New Haven: Yale University Press, 1979, pp. 386-403.
   2. Tversky, Amos, and Kahneman, Daniel, "Judgment Under Uncertainty: Heuristics and Biases," *Science,* Sept. 27, 1974, p. 1124.
   3. Secord, P. F., "Stereotyping and Favorableness in the Perception of Negro Faces, *Journal of Abnormal and Social Psychology,* 1959, p. 313.

212 After making a faulty: Temerlin, M., and Trousdale, W. W., "The Social Psychology of Clinical Diagnosis," *Psychotherapy; Theory, Research and Practice,* 1969, 6, pp. 24-29.

212 This partly irrational process: Tversky, Amos, and Kahneman, Daniel, *op. cit.*

212 There may be some: Dailey, C. A., "The Effects of Premature Conclusions Upon the Acquisition of Understanding of a Person," *Journal of Psychology,* 1952, 33, pp. 133-152.

213 We behave in ways: Farina, A., Allen, J. G., and Saul, B. B., "The Role of the Stigmatized Person in Affecting Social Relationships," *Journal of Personality,* 1968, 36, pp. 169-182.

214 Daniel Isenberg of Harvard: Isenberg, Daniel J., "How Senior Managers Think," *Harvard Business Review,* November-December 1984, pp. 81-90.

214 His description of how: Simon, Herbert A., *Models of Thought, op. cit.*

217 We are told by: Maltz, Maxwell, *Psycho-Cybernetics,* N. Hollywood, California: Wilshire Book Co., 1977, p. XXIII.

219 In the spring of: Gordon, Arthur, *Norman Vincent Peale,* Englewood Cliffs, New Jersey: Prentice-Hall, 1958, pp. 78-79. Reprinted by permission of Mr. Arthur Gordon.

AFTERWORD

My goal has been to provide you with all the information you need to be a better speaker than 90 percent of the people you know. If you feel I've been of service to you, I'd appreciate a short note describing your experiences in applying these methods and techniques. I will treasure it as a prized possession.

I plan occasionally to revise and update this book. If you have suggestions for improvement in any area, I would welcome them.

Finally, I will also be grateful for any ideas you may have about topics for other books or materials that would be helpful and of service to you or others.

To your success,

John L. Dutton
Route 1 — Kanaman Rd.
New London, WI 54961

"Obstacles are those frightful things
you see when you take your eyes
off your goals."
                    —Unknown

FOR FURTHER STUDY

If you want to read more, here are eight books that I recommend as worth at least a brief review. Not all of them are about public speaking, but each one could help you be a better speaker than most of the people you know.

Bartlett, John, *Bartlett's Familiar Quotations,* New York: Little Brown and Co., 1980.

Campbell, Cy, *Power And Influence Through Public Speaking,* West Nyack, N. Y.: Parker Publishing Co., 1972.

Fellman, Hazel, *The Best Loved Poems Of The American People,* Garden City, N. Y.: Garden City Books, 1936.

Jay, Antony, *The New Oratory,* New York: American Management Association, 1971.

Linkletter, Art, *Public Speaking For Private People,* New York: Bobbs-Merrill Co., 1980.

Linver, Sandy, *Speak Easy,* New York: Simon and Schuster, 1978.

Maltz, Maxwell, *Psycho-Cybernetics,* New York: Pockett Books, 1960.

Watson, Lillian E., *Light From Many Lamps,* New York: Simon and Schuster, 1951.

"You will become as small as your controlling desire; as great as your dominant aspiration."

—James Allen

INDEX

Acceptance and trust: how to gain, 49–51

Actor: in interview with psychiatrist, 27–28

Advertising: compared to speech content, 57

Advocacy speeches: topics for, 190

Affirmation: effect on audience, 38–39

Alda, Alan: quoted about making distinctions, 26

Analytical thinking: and human behavior, 211–214

Anniversaries: speeches for, 189

Answers for exercise, 152–153

Anxiety: sources, 172; effect of, 172

Attention, audience: how to keep from wandering, 54; how to regain, 56–57

Audience: how to "read," 191

Aun, Michael A.: and practice, 143

Bartlett, John: *Bartlett's Familiar Quotations,* 225

Becker, Ernest: quoted on meaning, 40

Behavior: irrational, a fact of life, 213–214; consistent with our reputation, 213

Beliefs and feelings: touched by stories, 73

Bemis, Dr. Warren: quoted on preferences for dedication, 90

Best Loved Poems Of The American People: book by Hazel Fellman, 225

Burnham, Daniel: quoted on planning, 215

Campbell, Cy: *Power and Influence Through Public Speaking,* 225

Carry over: as audience behavior, 27–28

Casual reading: as source of stories, 85

Chess: Simon's research described, 21–22

Church groups: topics of talks for, 189–190

Churchill, Sir Winston: poor speaker who improved, 14; practice techniques, 138; practice for impromptu speeches, 200

Clothing: what to wear, 115

Commitments, your personal: how to communicate, 54

Communication: hot versus cool, 55

Competition: effect of in meetings, 201

Conclusion, speech: design and effect of, 58, 59; final words in speech, 60

Conclusions: how people reach, 211–213

Content portion of speech: length of, 55; effect on audience, 56; compared to advertising, 57

227

ORDER FORM

LIFE SKILLS PUBLISHING COMPANY
P.O. BOX 282
NEW LONDON, WISCONSIN 54961

Please send me:

_____ copies of *How To Be An Outstanding Speaker*
by John L. Dutton @ $13.95 each.

Name: _____

Street: _____

City: _____

State: _____ Zip Code: _____

Wisconsin Residents: Please add 70 cents per book for sales tax.

Shipping: $1.00 for the first book; 25 cents for each additional
book.

_____ I can't wait 3–4 weeks for Book Rate. Here is
$2.50 per book for Air Mail.

Total Amount Enclosed: $_____

ORDER FORM

LIFE SKILLS PUBLISHING COMPANY
P.O. BOX 282
NEW LONDON, WISCONSIN 54961

Please send me:

_____ copies of *How To Be An Outstanding Speaker*
by John L. Dutton @ $13.95 each.

Name: _____

Street: _____

City: _____

State: _____ Zip Code: _____

Wisconsin Residents: Please add 70 cents per book for sales tax.

Shipping: $1.00 for the first book; 25 cents for each additional book.

_____ I can't wait 3–4 weeks for Book Rate. Here is $2.50 per book for Air Mail.

Total Amount Enclosed: $_____

ORDER FORM

LIFE SKILLS PUBLISHING COMPANY
P.O. BOX 282
NEW LONDON, WISCONSIN 54961

Please send me:

_____ copies of *How To Be An Outstanding Speaker*
by John L. Dutton @ $13.95 each.

Name: _____

Street: _____

City: _____

State: _____ Zip Code: _____

Wisconsin Residents: Please add 70 cents per book for sales tax.

Shipping: $1.00 for the first book; 25 cents for each additional
book.

_____ I can't wait 3–4 weeks for Book Rate. Here is
$2.50 per book for Air Mail.

Total Amount Enclosed: $_____

ORDER FORM

LIFE SKILLS PUBLISHING COMPANY
P.O. BOX 282
NEW LONDON, WISCONSIN 54961

Please send me:

_____ copies of *How To Be An Outstanding Speaker*
by John L. Dutton @ $13.95 each.

Name: _____

Street: _____

City: _____

State: _____ Zip Code: _____

Wisconsin Residents: Please add 70 cents per book for sales tax.

Shipping: $1.00 for the first book; 25 cents for each additional book.

_____ I can't wait 3–4 weeks for Book Rate. Here is $2.50 per book for Air Mail.

Total Amount Enclosed: $_____

4261-8
5-13